CEDAR GROVE CEMETERY INSCRIPTIONS

South Bend— St. Joseph County, Indiana

I0153541

Gene (Genevieve) Stachowiak Szymarek

HERITAGE BOOKS
2012

HERITAGE BOOKS
AN IMPRINT OF HERITAGE BOOKS, INC.

Books, CDs, and more—Worldwide

For our listing of thousands of titles see our website
at
www.HeritageBooks.com

Published 2012 by
HERITAGE BOOKS, INC.
Publishing Division
100 Railroad Ave. #104
Westminster, Maryland 21157

International Standard Book Numbers
Paperbound: 978-1-55613-038-0
Clothbound: 978-0-7884-9206-8

To my paternal grandparents,

Jan and Katarzyna Stachowiak,

who came here from Poland and rest here from their labors.

INTRODUCTION

To assist those who may encounter difficulties in reviewing these cemetery records, may I briefly explain the following:

A. The majority of names listed are from tombstones; these were painstakingly recorded by laboriously walking through the cemetery ground. In conjunction with these is a chronological listing of names taken from a conglomeration of assorted material that "fell into my hands"; therefore this may result in some error of Sections listed.

B. Realizing full well that the tombstones of Poles were inscribed in that beautiful, native language and that very few individuals can read or write same, all inscriptions have been translated except a few given names which are listed on the following page.

My deepest gratitude goes to my late husband, John F. Szymarek, who, prior to his death in 1982, assisted in all phases of this work. His encouragement brought this work to completion.

Gene (Genevieve) Szymarek
1987

POLISH GIVEN NAME TRANSLATIONS

F - Female   M - Male

Agnieszka	Agnes
Aleks	Alex
Alicya	Alice
Alfons	Alphonse
Aloysius	Al
Alojzy	Alex
Aniela	Angela
Antonina	Antonette
Apolonia	Pauline
Augusta	Used: Gusty
Boleslaw	William
Bronislaw	Bernard
Bronislawa	Bernice-Bertha
Eligius	Same-used Eli
Elzbieta	Elizabeth
Franciszek (M)	Frank-Francis
Franciszka (F)	Frances
Genowefa	Genevieve
Hedwige	Harriet-Hattie
Heronim	Jerome
Jadwiga	Harriet-Hattie
Jan	John
Jerzy	George (See: Wojciech)
Jozef	Joseph
Jozefa	Josephine
Karol	Carl
Karolina	Caroline
Katarzyna	Katharine
Kazimierz	Casimir
Kazimiera (F)	Casimiera
Konstanty (M)	Constant

Konstancia	Constance
Konstancya	Constance
Klemenc	Clement-Clem
Klementyna	Clementina
Kswary	Xavier
Leokadya	Lillian
Ludwik	Louis
Ludwika	Louise
Mateusz	Matthew
Mieczyslaw	Mitchel-used Matthew
Pawel	Paul
Pelegia	(No translation used: Blanche)
Piotr	Peter
Prakseda	(No translation used: Sadie)
Stanislaw	Stanley
Stanislawa	Stella
Szczepan	Steve-Stephen
Stefan	Stephen-Steven
Waclaw	Charles
Walarya	Valaria
Walentyna	Valentina
Wawrzyn	Lawrence
Wawrzyniec	Lawrence
Weron	Vern
Weronika	Veronica
Wincenty	Vincent
Wladyslaw (M)	Lott-Lottie
Wladyslawa (F)	Lottie
Wojciech	Adelbert (At times Edward or Albert was used but George was used by most)
Zofia	Sophia
Zuzanna	Susan-Susanna
Zygmund	Sigmond

ABBREVIATIONS

States have been abbreviated using the US postal codes.

Arty   Artillery
Bn   Battalion
Btry   Battery
Co   Company/County
Cpl   Corporal
CSC   Congregation of the Holy Cross, priests of
        Notre Dame, IN. The abbreviation is for
        the Latin name of the religious order.
CWT   possibly Chemical Warfare Technician
Div   Division
Eng   Engineer
FA   Field Artillery
Fld   Field
Hq   Headquarters
Inf   Infantry
Mach   Machine (Gun)
Maint   Maintenance
MM   Machinist Mate
nee   born
Ord   Ordinance
QM   Quartermaster
Pfc   Private first class
Pvt   Private
Regt   Regiment
S   Seaman
Sgt   Sargeant
Sq   Squad
Sup   Supply
Tec(h) Technician
USNR   Unites States Naval Reserve
vet   Veteran
WWI   World War I
WWII   World War II

CEMETERY INSCRIPTIONS

ABRAHAM, Alex 1854 - 17
Jul 1938 D
Anna 1876 - 23 Jan 1944 D
ABRAHAM, Anna 1854 - 5
Feb 1942 E
Barbara 1864 - 6 Mar 1943
E
ACKERMAN, Anna 1865 - 15
Jan 1940 C
ADAMCY, Wanda 1896 - 23
Feb 1965 C
ADELSPERGER, Nancy 1933
- 5 Oct 1941 A
ADELSPERGER,   Cecelia
1872 - 5 Feb 1942 B
Charles 1869 - 13 Dec 1944
B
ADER, Florian 1868 - 24 Jul
1940 C
Theresa 1867 - 31 Dec 1944
C
ALBEY, Frank 1895 - 1912 F
Joseph 1887 - 1928 F
ALDERFER, Martha 1886 -
16 June 1949 D
ALLEN, Robert Patrick 1931
- 1980 F "MM 1 US Navy
Korea"
Anna Marie 1889 - 1971 F
(Joseph S & Mary Szybo-
wicz, & Roman Bykowski
same lot)
ALLISON, Bertha 17 Dec
1894 - 1930 F "Wife of
Clarence Allison - nee:
Stachowiak" (Jan & Katar-
zyna Stachowiak same lot)

ANDA, Joseph S 1908 - 12
Apr 1973 B
ANDERSON, Wally 1887 - 14
Jul 1962 D
Jane 1924 - 14 Sept 1971 D
ANDERT, Anton J 1903 son -
3 Apr 1939 B
Mary C 1876 mother - 1931
B
Michael 1876 father - 15
Jul 1944 B
ANDERT, Elizabeth 1931 -
17 Jan 1944 D
ANDERT, Andrew 1899 fa-
ther - 1978 F
Elizabeth 1897 mother - 10
Oct 1917 F
ANDERT, Leo -no dates- H
ANDRAYCZAK, Antonina
1879 - 29 Apr 1940 E
(John Andrews same lot)
ANDREWS, John no date -
22 Oct 1947 "died at Los
Angeles, CA" (Antonina
Andrayczak same lot)
ANDRYSIAK, Waclaw Y -no
dates- "Co F 157 Ind Inf
Spanish American War" E
Frances X 1843 mother -
1926 E
Jacob 1840 father - 1931 E
Bruno P 1877 son - 1947 E
ANDRZEJEWSKI,   Martin
1865 father - 12 Dec 1951
C
Angela 1872 mother - 1935
(Nee: Szumski) (Michalina

1

ANDRZEJEWSKI (continued) & Karul Wetlant family same lot)

ANDRZEJEWSKI, Franciszek 1872 - 1898 B

Anna 1879 - 1899 B

Jedeth 1 month old 11 Jan 1942 B

ANDRZEJEWSKI, Maryanna 1821 - 26 Nov 1906 E (K Laskowski same lot)

ANDRZEJEWSKI, Wawrzyn 1842 - 1918 E

Jadwiga 1902 daughter - E (Jan, Maryanna, & Pelegia Jaworski same lot)

ANTAL, Peter -no dates- E (Stephen L, Steve, & Katalin Fabian same lot)

ANTOL, Katalin Fabian -no dates-

ARANOWSKI, Jacob 1864 - 14 Jun 1904 E

Helen 1873 - 3 Oct 1947 E

John C 1900 - 13 Oct 1963 E

ARANOWSKI, Anton 1852 - 1915 A

ARANOWSKI, Joseph J 18 Feb 1894 father - 15 Nov 1970 B "Ind Pvt US Army WWI"

Eugene 4 July 1920 son - B

Bernice May 1895 mother - 4 Apr 1971 B (Nee: Stachowiak)

ARMSTRONG, Alice J 1875 - 11 Feb 1951 B "died at Chicago, IL"

ARCH, Stephen 1868 - 7 Mar 1941 A

ARNDT, Mary J 1878 - 1898 A (Nee: Peterson) (Julia & Charles Peterson same lot)

ARNDT, Katharine 1854 mother - 8 Jan 1941 A "Wife of Frederick Arndt, Sr"

Harry J 12 Feb 1879 - 24 Mar 1921 (Anna & Ruth J Thomas same lot)

ARNDT, Caroline 23 Sept 1838 - 8 Jun 1905 D

Julius 1838 - 1922 D

ASKMAN, Michael 1860 - 3 Oct 1945 A "Died at Rhinelander, WI"

AUMAN, Paul 2 weeks old 3 Feb 1939 A

AVERY, Martha 1867 - 16 June 1949 F

AXNIT, Louis 1892 - 16 Mar 1946 A

BABICH, Stephen 1920 son and brother 1921 G

BABICZ, Frank 1903 - 2 Sept 1941 D

BACH, Anne 1887 - 22 May 1967 A

BADUR, John June 1858 father - 1928 A

Josephine June 1868 mother - 1933 (Nee: Bartoszek) A

Sally no dates A

BAGARUS, George 1887 - 8 July 1962 B

Barbara 1892 - 17 Aug 1947 B

BAGNER, Mary 1876 - 2 Dec 1967 C

BAILEY, Marie M 1889 - 9 Nov 1970 F

Charles W 1874 - 7 Dec 1938 F

BAIN, Theresa 1887 - 8 Aug 1959 B

L 1870 - 28 Apr 1956 B

BALKA, Steve 1876 - 1919 B

BALKA, Richard C 28 May 1930 - 19 Aug 1962 D (Andrzej, Agnieszka, & Kas-

2

BALKA (continued)
imierz Witucki same lot)
BALOUN, Michael 1878 - 6
Aug 1951 A (Jacob, Helen,
Leo, & Joseph Janowiak;
William & Michael North;
seph Wcisel; & Helen Ho-
sinski same lot)
BANACH, Leo 10 Apr 1921 -
12 Feb 1923 F (Frank &
Frances Szymczak same
lot)
BANACKI, see BANATZKI
BANATZKI, John 1844 -
1926 C
Tekla 1854 - 1927 C (Nee:
Kolaczynski) (Adolph &
Martha Humberger same
lot)
BARANY, Andrew 1894 - 15
Sept 1970 -
BARANYAI, Paul 1871 - 30
Jan 1946 C
Theresa 1884 - 21 Aug 1973
C
BARANYAI, Joseph 1871 - 1
Jan 1946 D
BARANYAI, Mary 1896 - 26
Aug 1946 A
BARANYAI, Elizabeth 1889 -
11 Nov 1957 A
BARANYAI, Barbara 1871 -
27 Apr 1949 C
BARBER, John R 1902 - 14
Mar 1972 C "Died at Bu-
chanan, MI"
Tillie 1877 - 4 Mar 1939 C
(Nee: Wesolowski)
John 1864 - 1949 C
Irene 1909 - 1913 C (Ed-
ward L, John, & Christian
Lechnorowicz same lot)
BARCOME, Parmelia 1873 -
2 Dec 1941 C
Stephen 1868 - 30 Nov 1962
C

BARCZA, Anna 1884 - 19
Jan 1940 E
Joseph S 1874 - 1934 E
Joseph Jr 1904 - 1925 E
(Josephine A Hack Coll-
ner same lot)
BARCZAK, Valentine 8 Sept
1886 - 8 Feb 1949 D (IN
Pvt Hq Co 6th Rgt FA RD
WWI) (Joanna, Max J &
Josephine Grams same
lot)
BARLIN, Allan 1886 - 6 Jan
1968 C
BARRETT, Orde 1881 - 11
Sept 1960 C
Mathilda 1878 - 23 Oct
1967 C
BARSHAW, Peter ? - 11 Nov
1938 F "Died at Bertrand,
MI"
BARTKOWIAK, Ignacy 1857
father - 1909 A
Jadwiga 1863 mother - 1934
A (Nee: Bucholtz)
BARTOL, Joseph A 1899 -
13 June 1971 A
Mary 1893 - 4 Apr 1940 A
BARTOL, Lawrence no dates
D
BARTOL, Stanley L 20 Apr
1896 - 11 Dec 1972 E
Anna C - 6 Feb 1894 - 19--
E (Nee: Kazmierczak)
BARTOSZEK, Bronislava
1862 - 19-- D
Wladyslaw 27 Jan 1857 -
20 Sept 1899 D
Salomea 1866 mother -
1937 D (Nee: Lisiecki)
BARTOSZEK, Joseph 23 Apr
1894 - 24 June 1968 D
Gertrude no dates D (Nee:
Sechowski)
BARTOSZEK, Joseph Jr 1921
- 1924 F (Anna Kalamaja

BARTOSZEK (continued) same lot)

BAUER, Ted 1882 - 18 June 1944 D

Robert J 1878 - 17 Mar 1941 D (Veronica Bauer Beck same lot)

BAUER, A 1877 - 19 Jan 1956 C

BAUER, Anna 1876 - 14 Nov 1966 C

BAUMBACK, Margaret 1866 - 5 June 1944 B

BAUMGARTNER, Helen 1880 - 1 Aug 1944 E

BEACH, Katharine A 1880 - 4 Mar 1951 F "Died at Lakewood, OH"

BECK, Veronica Bauer 1858 - 1921 D

George 1883 - 2 Oct 1953 D

Mary 1883 - 3 Nov 1952 D (Theodore & Robert Bauer same lot)

BECKRICH, Cecelia 1909 - 28 Feb 1959 D

BECZKIEWICZ, Tekla 5 Sept 1818 - 4 Sept 1894 A "Wife of Teofil Becz- kiewicz"

BECZKIEWICZ, Leonard 1905 - 1906 C (Note: obit in South Bend Tribune Newspaper reads Died 17 April 1904) (Francizska Rybicki same lot)

BEDEKER, A 1886 - 11 Nov 1956 -

BEDNAR, Anna 1874 - 1920 B

Anton 1871 - 27 Jan 1948 B

Cecelia 1870 - 24 July 1947 B

BEDNOROWICZ, Ignatius 1890 - 20 May 1941 E

BEDNOROWICZ, Katharine

BEDNOROWICZ (continued) 1890 wife - 25 Feb 1947 F "Died at Denver, CO" (Jan, Antonina, Michael, Antoni, & Wladyslawa Rajter same lot)

BELHUMEUR, Emma or Anna 1864 - 6 Oct 1939 C

BELLA, Andrew 1868 - 25 Sept 1942 F

BELEDIN, Elizabeth 1853 - 25 Nov 1940 F

BENITZ, William 1873 - 1 June 1942 B

BERES, George 1918 - 17 Dec 1968 -

BERFANGER, Anthony ? - 28 Mar 1970 B

F 1889 - 18 June 1955 B

BERFANGER, Leo 1927 - 22 Apr 1942 F

Rose 1908 - 26 May 1964 F

BERGAN, Cecelia 1918 - 21 June 1968 A "Died at San Pierre, IN"

John E 1909 - 10 Dec 1943 A

Cornelius 1916 - 30 May 1961 A

BERGAN, Rose 1878 - 11 Nov 1960 D

BERKOWSKI, Antonette 1866 - 13 Oct 1948 D

BERNDT, Joseph 1902 - 1902 E

Albert 1904 son - 1905 E

John 1879 father - 1955 E

Agnes 1886 mother - 1936 E

BERNER, Hilary 1900 - 221 Nov 1967 A "Died at Plainwell, MI"

Henry J 1868 - 27 Feb 1952 A

BERNHARDT, Webber 1873 - 11 Feb 1953 C "Died at

4

BERNHARDT (continued)
Barcien Springs, MI"
BEUNER, Joseph 1863 - 18
Feb 1951 A
BEVERELY, Marya 1877 -
19 June 1946 A
BEYER, Mary 7 Mar 1881 -
19 Apr 1960 (Nee: Paszek)
D
Jacob 1873 - no date D
Magdolene 1824 - 16 Apr
1900 D (Joseph Paszek &
Mary Pilarski Paszek
same lot)
BIENING, D 1868 - 19 Sept
1955 C "Died at Nobles,
IN"
BILINSKI, Anthony 28 Mar
1861 father - 1930 D
Antonette 1864 mother 1944
D
BIREN, Helen 1892 - 15 June
1962 E
BIRNER, Leo 1895 - 29 May
1968 A
Catharine 1861 - 4 Jan 1944
A
BISSELL, Josephine 1869 - 3
Mar 1950 C
BLACHA, Stephen 1881 - 18
Apr 1947 A
Kazimiera 1892 - 28 Mar
1952 A
BLADECKI, Matthew 1827 -
1909 C (Martin & Mary
Kwiatkowski same lot)
BOBOLENYI, Theresa 1886 -
19 Mar 1939 E
J 1881 - 30 Mar 1956 E
BOCK, Lenora 1864 - 14 Mar
1939 E
Frank J Sr 1858 - 6 Jan
1942 B
BOGAL, Ignatz 1872 - 5 Aug
1961 D
BOGUCKI, Victoria M Dec

BOGUCKI (continued)
1880 - 1917 (Nee: Marshal)
E "Wife of Antoni
Bogucki" (Piotr & Mary-
anna Niewiadomy; Frank &
Rose Ludwiczak same lot)
BOGUNIA, Walter P 1926 -
19-- C
Katharyn V 1921 - 1976 C
BOGUSZEWSKI, Stanley
1897 - 24 Nov 1954 E
BOINSKI, Bronislaw 3 Nov
1879 - 13 Sept 1898 A
Casimir 1888 - 24 Apr 1942
A "IN Cpl 334 Inf 84 Div"
Henry 3 Jan 1884 - 28 July
1884 A
BOINSKI, Julianna 1870 - 14
Mar 1950 C "Died at
Detroit, MI"
BOITS, Walter 1885 - 12 Jan
1960 D
BOJARSKI, Valentine no date
- 15 Aug 1928 C "Wife of
Frank Bojarski, Sr" (Nee:
Bonek)
BOLAND, Joseph 1905 - 26
Feb 1960 G
Margaret 1906 - 23 Feb
1966 G
BOLKA, Katharine 1841
mother - 1913 A
BONDA, John 1859 father - 5
May 1938 A
Catharine 1856 mother -
1930 A (Nee: Aranowski)
BORGERON, Armadore 1878
- 27 Feb 1952 F
BORKOWSKI, Victor D no
date - 27 Aug 1958 C
Jozef 1892 son - 1906 C
Jan 1850 father - 1921 C
Anna 1858 mother - 1931 C
(Nee: Mazurek)
Jack 1902 - 1958 C
John L 1879 father - 1954 C

5

BORKOWSKI (continued)
Catharine 1883 mother – 1938 C (Nee: Gramza)
Louise R 1910 daughter – 1935 C
BORLIK, Albin 1 Mar 1885 – 1968 C
Lottie 1885 mother – 5 June 1966 C (Nee: Jaworski)
BOROWSKI, J W 1880 – 4 Jan 1954 C
BOROWSKI, Charles C 1913 – 1979 D
A Evelyn 1914 – 19-- D
BORSOWICZ, see DYSKIE-WICZ BOROSOWICZ family
BORTS, Matilda 1892 – 13 Jan 1962 D "Married 30 May 1939"
BOSWORTH, Lucy 1868 – 22 Aug 1944 B
BOURDON, Joseph 1904 – 23 July 1965 C
Joseph H 1884 – 13 Jan 1949 C
BOYERS, S 1897 – 1930 D "M.D." (Hattie R, Stephen H, & Helen C Kubiak same lot)
BRADEN, Helen 1888 – 13 Mar 1973 D "Died at Ridgedale, NH" (Wozniak on same lot)
BRADY, Anna 1868 – 31 Mar 1943 B
Mary 1862 – 22 Aug 1947 B
Ella T 1872 – 2 Dec 1951 B
BRANNAN, Mary 1875 – 19 Mar 1945 D
Anna 1870 – 17 Oct 1946 D
Frank 1878 – 19 Nov 1946 D
Rose 1877 – 24 Mar 1953 D
"All died at Chicago, IL"
BRAUGBAL, W 1864 – 18 Aug 1956 – Community

BRAUGBAL (continued)
Cemetery at Notre Dame
BRAUNSDAY, William H 1869 – 24 Aug 1950 A
BRAUNSDORF, Karl 2 months old 9 July 1940 A
Robert 1899 – 7 Oct 1965 A
Mrs Wm H 1870 – 2 Jan 1951 A
BREHMER, Charles 1885 – 20 May 1962 A
BRENNAN, William 1865 – 4 June 1939 B
BRICHENSEN, Mary 1863 – 27 Apr 1949 C
BRISTOL, Mary 1865 – 14 Apr 1943 D
BROOKS, Don 1934 – 17 Mar 1973 –
BROSK, Stanley Joseph 7 Sept 1891 – 1 Apr 1957 H "IN 1st Sgt Co L 7 Inf Regt WWI"
BROSSARD, Emma 1870 – 12 Mar 1941 A "Died at Chicago, IL"
BROTHERS, Helen 1907 – 4 Oct 1959 C
BROWN, Emma 1892 – 16 July 1969 A "Died at Anaheim, CA"
Cathleen no date – 17 Dec 1949 A
BROWSER, Tillie J 1907 – 20 Mar 1973 – "Died at Elkhart, IN"
BROYLES, Cecelia no dates C (Steven & Amelia Lasicki same lot)
BRUGGNER, Rose no date – 10 June 1969 –
BRUGGNER, John 1866 – 1 June 1942 C
Johanna 1868 – 23 Aug 1959 C
BRUGGNER, Paulinia 1870 –

BRUGGNER (continued)
27 May 1947 F
BRUNSON, Ethel J 1905 - 30
June 1950 -
BRZECZYNSKI, Szczepan 24
Dec 1835 father - 10 May
1902 D
BRZEZINSKI, Wojciech 1816
grandfather - 1912 D
Wincenty Sr 13 Dec 1862
father - 13 Dec 1934 D
Anna 1864 mother - 26 Dec
1948 (Nee: Nowak) D
BRZEZINSKI, Michal Sept
1857 father - 1922 D
Aloysius 1899 son - 1933 D
Frances Sept 1859 mother -
no date D (Nee: Secula)
BUCKLEY, James 1886 - 20
Sept 1961 A
Mary 1873 - 21 Oct 1958 A
(Both died at Tampa, FL)
BUCKLEY, Mina 1885 - 21
Aug 1946 C "Died at Wau-
watosa, WI"
BUCKLEY, James W 1883 -
18 Jan 1942 D "Died at
Logansport, IN"
BUCZKOWSKI, Jozef 1872 -
1916 D
Ludwig 1841 - 1922 D
Leokadya 1852 - 1928 D
(Nee: Palicki) (Stella
Cwiklinski same lot)
BUCZKOWSKI, Julia 1863 -
11 Apr 1938 D
Anna T 27 Nov 1888 - 8
May 1971 D
BUCZKOWSKI, Katharine J
26 Feb 1894 - 10 June
1979 E
John 1855 father - 1931 E
BUDNIK, Anna 1873 - 7 Apr
1969 F (Nee: Woodka)
Nicholas J 1870 - 5 Aug
1963 F

BUDNIK, Marcin 1857 - no
date D
Katarzyna 1836 - 1927 D
Marya 1866 - 1923 D
BUDNIK, Eugene 2 June 1934
- 10 June 1934 E
BUDZIAK, no names & no
dates (4) iron crosses D
BUDZINSKI, Pelegia 1862 -
1896 F
Martin 1862 - 1916 F
Josephine 1879 - 31 Oct
1958 F
Leo J 21 Aug 1895 - 23 Jan
1973 F "Pvt Co A 142 Inf
WWI"
Konstanty 1898 - 1963 F
BUECHE, Kenneth F 1910 -
27 May 1969 - "Died at
Niles, MI"
Celeste P no date - 12 Aug
1969 -
Agnes 1885 - 2 Jan 1940 -
BUIPSE, R 1893 - 23 Dec
1955 D
BUKOWSKI, Wojciech 17
Mar 1856 - 18 Feb 1920 D
Antonina 1966 - 13 Oct
1948 D (Nee: Mnichow-
ski)
Stanley 1890 - 27 July 1946
D
BUKOWSKI, Clara L 1927 -
1928 F
Clarence 2 Nov 1927 - 18
May 1952 F "Pfc 32 Inf 7
Inf Div Korean Vet"
Julius I 1897 - 7 Sept 1979
F "Pvt US Army WWI"
BULMANSKI, Leon 1871 -
1910 E
Franciszek 1894 - 1895 E
Mary K 8 Aug 1880 - 11
Mar 1951 E (Nee: Taber-
ski) (Pelegia, Maryanna, &
Wladyslaw Taberski same

7

BULMANSKI (continued)
lot)
BUNBURY, Frank 1878 - 21
Oct 1941 D
Rose 1884 - 4 Feb 1964 D
"Died at Niles, IL"
Mollie 1906 - 15 Aug 1959
D
BUNDA, John 1859 - 5 May
1938 A
Catharine 1856 - 1930 A
(Nee: Aranowski)
BURNS, Marie J 1894 - 2
Aug 1969 -
BURNS, Ollie 1898 - 24 Dec
1958 C
BURNS, Charles 1895 - 29
May 1952 D
BUSCH, Carrie 1858 - 7 Dec
1946 B
Louise 1891 - 30 Jan 1941
B "Both died at Chicago,
IL"
BUSCZKY, Maria M 10 Aug
1911 - 1911 H
BUTLER, William 1894 - 4
Dec 1939 A
Paul 1906 - 30 Dec 1962 A
Mary 1867 - 17 Feb 1961 A
BUTLER, Goldie 1890 - 26
July 1960 D
BUZOLITS, John 1862 - 21
Apr 1946 A
Mary 1862 - 30 June 1952 A
BYKOWSKI, Roman 1865 - 9
Nov 1904 F
Frank 1862 father - 7 May
1944 F
Magdaline 1859 mother -
1936 F (Anna Maria Allen
same lot)
CABANAW, B 1895 - 6 Aug
1954 D
CALLAHAN, John E 1866 -
8 Apr 1951 A "Died at
Hammond, IN"

CAREY, Rev Wm A 1867 - 3
June 1947 Community
Cemetery ND
CASASANTA, Joseph J 1901
- 1 Dec 1968 -
CASEY, George Henry 1891 -
15 May 1969 -
CASEY, Mary J 1865 - 2
June 1949 B
Cecelia 1862 - 25 Feb 1939
B
CASEY, Lucy 1867 - 13 Dec
1940 C "Died at Cleve-
land, OH"
CASEY, Catharine 1870 - 21
May 1948 D
CASEY, Mary 1880 - 1 Nov
1942 F
CASH, Edmund L 1890 - 31
Mar 1967 A "Died at CA"
Albert A 1881 - 28 Apr 1970
A
CASHEN, Vera 1901 - 14
Mar 1940 G
CASHEN, Sylvester W 1902
- 7 Mar 1950 C
CASIMIR, John V 1881 -
1924 D
Cecelia 1870 - 19 Feb 1963
D
Peter 1873 - 1906 D
Anthony 1876 - 1904 D
Albert Benedict 1845 father
1936 D
Victoria 1842 mother - 1886
D
James F 1908 - 21 Aug
1966 D
CAVANAUGH, Rev no name
1916 - 11 Nov 1954 Com-
munity Cemetery ND
CEGIELSKI, Michael 1863
father - 1910 E
Sophia 1871 mother - 13
Jan 1948 E (Nee: Kala-
maja) (Mary Ciegielski

CEGIELSKI (continued)
Rozewicz same lot)
CELESTINE, Bro no name
1874 - 31 Nov 1946 Com-
munity Cemetery ND
CELMER, Mary Nov 1871 -
1900 C (Nee: Rozwarski)
Frank July 1862 - 21 July
1942 C "Died at Detroit,
MI"
CERTIA, J 1875 - 26 Aug
1954 C
Mary 1860 - 22 Dec 1942 C
CHAUSE, Maurice 1879 - 28
Jan 1964 G
CHELMINIAK, Mary 1880 -
25 Apr 1968 C "Died at
LaHalesa, CA"
CHELMINIAK, Matthew T
1897 - 13 Mar 1947 D
Wladyslawa 1867 - 20 July
1954 D (Nee: Kucharski)
Adalbert G 1858 - 1 Apr
1942 D
CHELMINIAK, Jozefa 1888
daughter - 6 Dec 1918 D
Antonina 1861 - 23 Jan
1915 D (Nee: Bajer)
Wawrzyniec 1860 - 3 Oct
1922 D
CHEPARO, J 1889 - 12 July
1954 C
CHIONITZ, no name 1878 -
7 May 1963 E
CHIRHART, E 1870 - 7 July
1955 B
CHISZAR, Vera 1883 - 30
May 1967 C
Anna 1901 - 16 Feb 1969 C
CHIZAR, Mike 1913 - 25
June 1968 E
Omar 1901 - 16 Jan 1970 E
A 1879 - 14 Apr 1954 E
CHIZAR, Anna no date - 30
July 1938 A
CHLEBEK, Franciszka 1859

CHLEBEK (continued)
- 1 Aug 1901 E
Anastasia 1892 - 1911 E
Walentyna 1852 - 1920 E
CHODZINSKI, Peter J 15
June 1898 - 7 Oct 1958 D
"IN Pfc 80 Eng Water Sup
Bn WWII" (Joseph Rom-
secki same lot)
CHOKA, Joseph G 1883 - 20
Apr 1941 A
CHROBOT, Frank 1893 -
1894 D
Mack N 1897 - 11 July 1950
D
Harriet T 1893 - 31 Jan
1960 D (Nee: Ciesiolka)
Joseph 1869 - 6 Oct 1943 D
CHROBOT, Sadie 1863 - 23
Nov 1956 E (Nee: Jaros-
zewski)
Frank C 12 Nov 1888 - 25
Apr 1949 E "IN Pvt 158
Depot Brigade"
Joseph no dates E
CIESIELSKI, Stella L 1881 -
19 Mar 1951 F
Florence 1884 - 30 June
1969 F
Paul 1842 father - 21 July
1912 F
Frances 1846 mother - 1906
F (Nee: Krzyzaniak)
Lucya 1878 - 1895 F (B
Kurek same lot)
CIESIELSKI, Ludwika 1862 -
1934 E
CIESIELSKI, Matthew 1908
son - 24 Feb 1946 E
Mary 1878 mother - 1936 E
(Nee: Burkowski)
Thomas 1873 father - 1934
E
CIESIELSKI, Napomucena no
dates mother D
Szymon no dates father D

9

CIESIELSKI (continued)
Jozef no dates husband D
Maryanna no dates wife D
CIESIOLKA, Joseph 1902 - 1903 A
Irene 1903 - 1917 A
Stella E 1882 mother - 18 May 1967 A (Nee: Rudynski)
Ignatius 1877 father - 27 May 1950 A
CIESIOLKA, Pelegia 1866 - 16 June 1954 E (Nee: Mnichowski)
Franciszek 1863 - 1933 E
Matthew 1909 - 24 Feb 1946 E (Eliguis Kaminski same lot)
CINKOWSKI, Anne 1852 mother - 1922 C (Nee: Witucki)
John 1844 father - 1915 C
Valentine 1881 - 21 Nov 1952 C WWI
Josephine 1889 - 16 May 1965 C
CUIPINSKI, no name & no dates E
CLARK, Elizabeth B 1906 - 3 Oct 1950 C
CLAVES, Emil 1882 - 22 Apr 1962 -
CLAYTON, Clara 1899 - 5 May 1973 C
CLIFFORD, Margaret 1862 - 16 May 1941 A
COLLINS, Francis 1909 - 14 Dec 1961 G
COLLNER, Josephine A Hack 1922 - 1965 E (Anna, Joseph S, & Joseph Jr Barcza same lot)
CONDON, W 1869 - 7 May 1955 Community Cemetery ND
COOK, Lottie 1886 - 7 Dec

COOK (continued)
1949 A "Died at Chicago, IL"
COOK, Joseph Wm 1884 - 27 Sept 1966 C
Bertha 1889 - 30 Oct 1945 C
Lucy 1880 - 29 Aug 1944 C
COOK, Richard Daniel no date - 31 Jan 1937 E "MI Sgt 346 Bn Tank Corp" (Lawrence Sowala; Ladislaus & Mary Kruk; & Stephen K Gish same lot)
COONEY, Mrs M 1881 - 9 Sept 1941 A
L 1873 - 11 June 1954 A
Jerome 1862 - 25 Apr 1939 A
COQUILLARD, Maude 1854 - 19 Aug 1947 A
Elsie 1872 - 27 Feb 1949 A
Frances 1868 - 27 July 1949 A
COSGROVE, Frank 1886 - 17 Apr 1943 B
COTTRELL, George 1884 - 6 Nov 1948 D
COUCH, Cecylia M 1891 - 1974 B
Fred J 1888 - 30 June 1975 B
Joseph 4 June 1920 Son - 23 June 1920 B
COURTNEY, Marie 1908 - 27 July 1969 B "Died at Michigan City, IN"
COYLE, M 1894 - 21 Jan 1957 -
CREPEAU, Elton 1892 - 16 Mar 1949 A
CREPEAU, Anna 1900 - 22 Feb 1948 C
CRESSY, Sidney 1880 - 6 Sept 1960 A
Marie 1889 - 3 Oct 1961 A

10

CRESSY (continued)
Suzanne 1 day old - 7 Aug 1944 A
Fredice 1893 - 14 Mar 1961 A
CRESSY, Cecelia no date - 24 May 19-- (not legible) G
CRESSY, Clement 1885 - 3 Sept 1970 -
CRESSY, Ralph no date - 25 Dec 1972 -
CROWLEY, Henrietta 1878 - 5 Aug 1949 A "Died at Chicago, IL"
CROWLEY, Jerome 1877 - 19 Dec 1952 A "Died at Chicago, IL"
CROWLEY, William 1 month old - 6 Aug 1941 A
CSABI, Theresa 1879 - 8 May 1951 G
Stephen 1879 - 13 Apr 1946 G
CSARPER, Teresa 1894 - 8 Jan 1962 D
CSASZAR, Joseph 1867 - 23 Feb 1943 B
CSERNITS, Helen 1905 - 8 Dec 1944 E
CSISZAR, Mary 1886 - 11 Jan 1966 A
CUFF, Larry 1873 - 10 Aug 1944 -
CULHANE, Catharine 1894 - 15 Dec 1949 A
CULLINANE, Patrick 1910 - 16 July 1964 A
Patrick 1873 - 30 Mar 1945 A "Both died at Chicago, IL".
CUMMINGS, Margaret 1879 - 18 Jan 1944 C
CURRAN, Florence 1888 - 28 July 1971 - "Died at Buchanan, MI"

CURRAN, Mary Ann 1872 - 2 Nov 1950 C "Died at Evanston, IL"
CURTIS, Stephen A Sr 1891 - 5 Jan 1969 -
Marian D 1896 - 14 Nov 1971 -
CWIKLINSKI, Stella 1880 - 26 Jan 1967 D (Nee: Buczkowski) (Jozef Buczkowski same lot)
CWIKLINSKI, Nikodem 1874 - 1891 D
Konstancya 1850 - 1928 D (Nee: Andrzejewski)
Jan 1845 - 1929 D
Alexander 2 Feb 1889 - 23 Mar 1931 D "IN Pvt 7 Inf 3rd Div"
CYBART, Angeline 1865 - 25 Mar 1950 D (nee: Kolczynski)
Stanley 1854 - 26 Apr 1941 D
Marcyanna 1818 - 1884 D
Delena no dates D
Antoni no dates D
CYBART, Jan 1845 - 1917 A
Joanna 1839 - 4 Jan 1911 A (Jozefa Wojciechowski same lot)
CYLKA, Julia B Wentland 2 Sept 1902 - 16 July 1978 F (Nee: Tuligowski) (Joseph L Wentland same lot)
CZAJKOWSKI, Jan no dates D
Anna no dates D (Nee: Kendziorski)
CZAKLER, N 1882 - 13 Jan 1955 G
Jennie 1889 - 13 Aug 1958 G
CZARNECKI, infant 1 day old - 1 Nov 1940 -

CZERNA, Theresa 1902 - 3 Dec 1957 G

CZERWINSKI, John 1909 - 1920 C (Leon T Kindt same lot)

CZOSNOWSKI, Julia K 1872 mother - 24 Feb 1949 C (Nee: Wesolowski) Joseph 1870 - father 1957 C (Walter F & Mary M Geabler same lot)

DAKAS, Theresa 1885 - 28 Jan 1958 C

DANKOWSKI, Wawrzyn no date - 1909 F Julianna no date - 1924 F

DAVELINE, Julia 1874 - 17 Feb 1961 F

DAVIS, Naomi 1895 - 6 Apr 1973 -

DEBUYSSER, Stella 1884 - 18 Apr 1967 C "Died at Elkhart, IN"

DECKER, Robert 1863 - 24 Sept 1942 E

DECLERQ, Clementine 1878 - 4 Oct 1963 C Emil 1887 - 17 July 1962 C

DEFREESE, C 1887 - 3 July 1953 C

DEGEYTER, Elsie 1914 - 3 May 1961 G

DEGOVITS, Sebastian A 1867 - 21 Mar 1951 E

DEGRAFF, Carmel 1900 - 11 Nov 1965 B Robert N 4 weeks old - 18 Aug 1964 B

DEGRAFF, ONeal 1895 - 1 Aug 1973 -

DEGRAFF, Ralph 1897 - 5 Oct 1957 C

DEGRAFF, William 1877 - 8 Aug 1939 D Thomas 1888 - 12 June 1963 D

DEGRAFF (continued) Horace 1878 - 10 July 1958 D

DEGRAFF, Emma 1874 - 13 Dec 1957 F "Died at Dowagiac, MI"

DEGROOTE, John F 1935 - 5 Sept 1938 D "Died at Rolling Prairie, IN"

DEGROOTE, Catharine 1871 - 21 Oct 1959 D Felix A 1874 - 27 May 1947 D

DEGROOTE, Rev John 1866 - 16 Oct 1946 Community Cemetery ND

DEKA, Alvin J 1917 - 13 Apr 1960 C Ann M 1925 - 19-- C Veronica 1875 - 1935 C John 1875 - 21 Dec 1957 C

DEKA, Leo 1885 - 2 Aug 1947 D Rose 1885 - 1925 D (Nee: Manuszak) Loretta M 1921 - 1 Oct 1972 D

DEKA, John 1851 - 1938 F Anna 1854 - 1932 F (Nee: Klewin) (Ignacy & Marta Niedzielski same lot)

DEKA, Ludwik 1855 - 26 Mar 1903 F Apolonia 1860 - 2 June 1921 F (Nee: Donarski) Jozef no dates F Cecyl no dates F Stanley 1895 - 9 Feb 1967 F Helen no dates F

DEMBKIEWICZ, Cecelia 21 Nov 1886 - 26 Jan 1962 D Douglas Stephen 1905 father - 1979 D

DEMSKI, Jacob 1880 - 23 Jan 1940 F

DEMSKI (continued)
Mary 1869 - 14 May 1945 F
(Nee: Kwiatkowski)
DEMSKI, Stanislaw 1881 -
1934 D
Constance 1882 - 21 Feb
1946 D (Nee: Szudrowicz)
Joseph infant son no dates
D
DEMSKI, Wojciech 1854 -
1901 F
Katarzyna 1864 - 1922 F
(Nee: Pilarski)
DENNIS, Bro no name 1882 -
22 Sept 1946 Community
Cemetery ND
DENTZ, Margaret 1866 - 19
May 1948 F
DEPPERT, Mary 1884 - 10
Aug 1959 E
A 1883 - 1 Sept 1955 E
DERANEK, Erwin 10 Dec
1919 - 14 June 1920 B
Vincent 13 Oct 1895 - 1923
B
Bernice 1897 - 1925 B
(Nee: Wozniak)
Esther 1916 - 1935 B
DERUYCK, Jeanette 1861 -
26 July 1947 C
DESITS, Joseph F 1908 - 27
Feb 1940 C
Rose 1886 mother - 2 July
1962 C (Nee: Martinski)
Joseph Sr 1876 father - 29
May 1959 C
John 1883 - 1930 C
Anna 1882 mother - 1914 C
(nee: Michocza)
DETZLER, Anna 1864 - 29
Feb 1948 D "Died at Elm-
hurst, IL"
DEUTSCH, Lawrence 1877 -
23 June 1969 -
DEVER, C 1884 - 20 Aug
1955 A

DEWALLE, Camille 1884 -
25 Dec 1940 C
DEWINNE, Peter 1871 - 22
June 1950 -
DEWITT, Camiel 1876 - 18
Apr 1950 B
Charlotte 1 day old - 12
Nov 1949 B
DEWYZE, Gentiel 1891 - 29
June 1959 E
E 1895 - 6 Nov 1956 E
DEYERLING, Benedict 1890
- 3 May 1961 A
DEYERLING, Anna A 1901 -
20 Feb 1957 C
Anne 1887 - 14 Apr 1947 C
DIAMOND, A 1882 - 22 Sept
1954 C
Beatrice 1884 - 15 May
1943 C
DIETZ, Mary 1850 - 1916 B
Michael 1856 - 1915 B
Edward J 1891 - 1962 B
Theora Miltenberger 1906 -
1971 B
DIETZ, no name 1876 mother
1907 A
Anna no dates A
Hugh A 1897 - 1948 A (Lil-
lian K Wensatt same lot)
DIGNAN, Francis 1872 - 5
Apr 1940 B "Died at Niles,
MI"
DISH, Matilda 1875 - 3 Oct
1951 A
Edward 1871 - 5 Mar 1943
A
DOBBELAERE, Emiel 1865
- 15 Apr 1945 D
DOBRZYKOWSKI, Wladys-
law 26 Sept 1877 - 5 Mar
1896 F (Stanislawa &
Franciszek Mozynski
same lot)
DOBRZYKOWSKI, Jan W
1852 - 1 Aug 1905 D (Mary

13

DOBRZYKOWSKI (continued)
Kruzel same lot)
DOKTOR, Louis 1896 - 1914
C
Michael 1856 father - 1927
C
Maryanna 1859 mother -
1934 C (Nee: Chwalek)
DOLL, Mary 1858 - 18 Nov
1939 D "Died at Milwau-
kee, WI"
DOMBKIEWICZ, S Dean 21
Nov 1935 - 20 Nov 1941 E
(Helen, Mary, & John Red-
ling; no name Zgod-
zinski; Bert & Josephine
Magiera; & Helen Wolt-
man same lot)
DOMBOS, Andrew 1856 -
1925 C
Louise 1875 mother - 11
Oct 1941 C
DOMBROWSKI, Max 1887 -
1 June 1948 C
Sophie 1885 - 20 Aug 1960
C (Marlene S Schroff same
lot)
DOMINICK, John Jr Sept
1839 - 1914 F
Christine July 1842 - 1910
F
Katharine Ann 1954 - 1978
F
DOMINSKI, Felix 1875 -
1906 A (Henrietta Fill; &
Frances & Stanley Szcza-
pinski same lot)
DONAHUE, George 1888 - 19
Feb 1962 D "Died at Los
Angeles, CA"
DONAHUE, John 1884 - 26
Nov 1939 D "Died at Ply-
mouth, IN"
DONOVAN, Michael 1867 -
24 Mar 1939 A
DONOVAN, Daniel 1869 - 20

DONOVAN (continued)
Aug 1945 Community
Cemetery ND (Brother Leo
was his clerical name)
DORAN, Margaret 1885 - 24
Aug 1953 C
William 1889 - 10 Apr 1961
C
DORN, John no date - 6 Jan
1940 C
DORRENBACHER, Frank
1864 - 23 Feb 1941 B
Dorothea 1864 - 17 Sept
1942 B
DORSCH, Barbara 1866 - 20
Sept 1943 F
DOWNS, Joseph F 1895 - 30
Nov 1943 A
Anna 1878 - 27 Dec 1946 A
Mary 1887 - 31 Mar 1972 A
DRADA, Agnes 1884 mother
- 1928 E
Albert F 1882 father - 12
Oct 1954 E
Violet M 1911 daughter - 26
June 1964 E
Joseph E 1908 son - 1973 E
DRAJUS, Joanna 1879 - 21
Feb 1959 D (Nee: Paces-
ny)
Martin J 13 Oct 1886 - 26
May 1952 D
DRAJUS, Andrew 1823 - 1918
C
Antonina 1830 - 1917 C
(Nee: Bilinski) (Michael &
Jozefa Klysz same lot)
DRAPEK, Stella Weise 1899
- 1974 F
John S 1897 - 4 June 1955
F
Catharine Dutriux 1895 -
1945 F
Petronella 1865 mother -
1933 F
Franciszek 1867 father -

DRAPEK (continued)
1918 F
DRASKOVITS, Frank 1877 –
3 Jan 1960 A
DRAVIS, William 1876 – 27
Oct 1946 D
DRAZSNYAK, Sophie 1885
mother – 1974 B
Joseph 1882 – 28 May 1966
B
Jacques 1910 – 1960 B
DREIBELBIS, Mary 1872 – 9
July 1960 D
Wm H 1870 – 15 Feb 1947
D
DREIBELBIS, Mary no date –
7 Sept 1949 F
DREJER, Pelegia 1881
mother – 19 Jan 1953 A
"Died at Des Moines, IA"
(Nee: Szamecka)
Francis J 1878 father –
1914 A
DREJER, Joseph F no dates
D
DREW, Mary 1886 – 10 Dec
1946 B
Ella 1894 – 10 Dec 1955 B
DUDIK, Leslie 1904 – 26
July 1940 F "Died at
Niles, MI"
Anna 1906 – 19–– F
DUGGAN, Arthur 1882 – 5
May 1953 D
DUKAI, Theresa 1857 – 4 Apr
1938 C
DUKAI, Joseph 1905 – 6 Aug
1947 C
DUKAR, J 1881 – 16 DEC
1953 C
DULY, Edward J no date – 11
June 1962 B
DUTRIEUX, Adolph 1879 –
13 Dec 1965 B
DUTRIEUX, Marion 1894 –
19 Dec 1952 B "Died at

DUTRIEUX (continued)
Hines, IL"
DUTRIEUX, Lena 1882 – 21
July 1965 B
Leo 1883 – 12 May 1952 B
Mary 1889 – 1 Mar 1959 B
DUTRIEUX, Katharine 1894 –
24 Oct 1945 F
DWORECKI, Franciszek Oct
1882 father – 6 May 1946
D
Jozefa 1884 – 1962 D (Nee:
Was)
DWYER, James 1879 – 26
Feb 1951 G
DYSKIEWICZ – BORSO-
WICZ family, Clementine
dates not legible F
Ignacy 1893 – 4 Feb (year
not legible) F
Antony 1894 – not legible F
EARL, Francis 1919 – 14 Jan
1941 A
Thomas A 1878 – 31 Mar
1953 A
EARL, Genevieve 1884 – 27
May 1959 C "Wife of
Thomas A Earl"
EBLE, Fred 1883 – 25 Aug
1942 – "Died at Cleve-
land, OH"
EBLE, Katharine E 1882 – 1
May 1961 C
Maximillian 1880 – 12 June
1961 C
Beatrice 1911 – 1912 C
EBLE, Franciszka 1850 –
1901 C
Ignatz 1849 – 1902 C
ECKENROTH, Joseph 1884 –
6 Jan 1965 D
EGIERSKI, Anna 1858 mother
– 1930 E
Wojciech 1856 father –
1911 E
EGRESCES, Carrie 1878 – 7

EGRESCES (continued)
Mar 1958 D
Paul 1879 - 14 May 1961 D
EGYHAZI, Nancy no date - 1
Mar 1943 -
EICHSTADT, E A 1858 - 8
Jan 1945 D
Mary 1866 - 10 Mar 1953 D
EICHSTADT, Anna 1885 - 27
June 1946 A
John 1912 son - 14 Feb
1964 A
Joseph 1877 father - 12 Feb
1964 A
ELLI, Alexander 1869 - 3
June 1947 G
ELLIS, Dwan 1 day old - 22
July 1938 E
EMERY, Everet F 1907 - 10
Jan 1950 D
ERHARDT, Clem 1890 - 2
Sept 1938 A
EVANS, Marie 1882 - 1924 A
"Wife of John W Evans -
married 20 May 1920" (Ri-
chard F Wisniewski same
lot)
EWING, Julius 1893 - 23
Sept 1946 A
FABIAN, Stephen L 6 Nov
1906 - 25 Jan 1972 E "IN
Pfc US Army WWII"
Steve 1876 - 2 May 1961 E
Katalin 1883 - 29 June 1970
E (Peter & Katalin Fabian
Antol same lot)
FABIANKOWICZ, Zigmond
1883 - 18 May 1970 H
C Gizella 1887 - 1918 H
FABIANOWICZ, Louise 1873
- 7 May 1966 C
FAHEY, Christopher 9 hours
old - 21 Oct 1966 A
FAHEY, Michael 1872 - 10
Aug 1944 -
FARKAS, Elizabeth 1864 -

FARKAS (continued)
30 Apr 1939 C
FARKAS, Velma 1870 - 28
Dec 1945 F
FARLEY, Anna 1869 - 14
May 1945 B
FARRAR, Michael 20 days
old - 3 Aug 1971 -
FARREL, Anne 1864 - 13
Sept 1938 B
FEARKES, John M 1888 - 17
Jan 1953 D "Died at
Hines, IL"
Katharine 1876 - 21 June
1944 D
FEKETE, Eleanor 1878 - 21
June 1966 C
FELIX, Frances T 1863 - 1
Feb 1946 C
FENTON, Mary 1874 - 24
Mar 1943 B
FEZY, Joseph J 1916 - 1977
C "Pvt US Army WWII"
(Lillian Nowakowski &
Joseph Luczkowski same
lot)
FILL, Henrietta Dominski no
dates A "Wife of Michael
Fill" (Felix Dominski;
Frances & Stanley Szcza-
pinski same lot)
FINCH, Edward D 1868 - 12
Jan 1953 C
FINNAN, Richard 1 day old -
17 Apr 1940 D
FINNERAN, John no date -
23 July 1973 -
FINNERAN, F X 1892 - 9
Oct 1945 A
FISCHER, Herman 1847 -
1900 C
Magdelena 1847 - 1925 C
Albert 1887 - 1923 C
Margaret Fisher Tusing
1872 - 1949 C
FISHER, Marion 1900 - 6

16

FISHER (continued)
Jan 1959 D
FITZPATRICK, infant 1 day
old - 13 Sept 1940 -
FITZSIMMONS, Gerald 1947
- 27 Mar 1971 -
FLAHERTY, James W 1916
- 24 July 1938 D
FLORKOWSKI, Stanley 1877
- 24 June 1944 C
Cecelia 1879 - 1960 C
(Nee: Jaworski)
FLOWERS, Michael 1870 -
1935 A
Frank 14 June 1897 - 14
Oct 1906 A
Blanche 1874 - 1943 A
Antony J 1893 - 17 Oct
1947 A
FLYNN, H 1885 - 18 Feb
1954 D "Died at Austin,
TX"
FLYNN, O 1887 - 19 Oct
1958 C "Died at Chicago,
IL"
FODOR, Theresa 1872 - 8
June 1949 C
FOLEY, J 1870 - 29 Jan
1956 -
FORSTER, Margaret 1875 -
21 Feb 1951 E
A 1900 - 24 July 1954 E
J 1872 - 3 Apr 1955 E
FOSTER, Matilda 1867 - 4
Apr 1951 A
George 1864 - 9 July 1947
A
FOSTER, Neville 1891 - 4
Jan 1973 -
FOSTER, Mary Chissim 1891
- 17 Aug 1966 H "Died at
Rocky River, OH"
FOY, John 1881 - 11 May
1972 -
FRAHLER, Mary 1860 - 19
Apr 1939 D "Wife of Mi-

FRAHLER (continued)
chael Frahler"
FRANKIEWICZ, Stella 1882
- 21 Oct 1969 C (Nee:
Wozniak)
Nicholas 1875 - 1 Feb 1952
C
FRANKLIN, C 1873 - 21 Mar
1956 B "Died at Buch-
anan, MI"
Martha 1873 - 22 Jan 1958
B
FRANKOWIAK, Marcela
1862 mother - 1928 A
George 1851 father - 1929 A
FRANKOWSKI, Carrie 1888 -
14 Mar 1968 -
FRANKOWSKI, Elizabeth 30
June 1913 - 27 Mar 1940 D
Art 1892 - 1 Sept 1962 D
Martha 8 July 1880 - no
date D (Nee: Pulcinski)
Antony 10 May 1892 - 1
Sept 1962 D
FREDERIK, Emery J 1895 -
28 Apr 1941 A "IN Pfc QM
Corps"
Emery A Jr 19 Apr 1926
Baby - 22 June 1927 A
(John & Agnes Niedbalski
same lot)
FREDERICK, Mary 1893 - 4
Mar 1939 A
Alex 1880 - 11 Mar 1943 A
FREDERICK, John 1866 -
1931 A
Rose 1876 Wife - 1932 A
Victor no dates Baby A
Alex 26 May 1912 - 29 Apr
1964 A
FREEMAN, William 1 day
old - 9 Dec 1939 B
FREEMAN, N 1871 - 5 Sept
1953 D
FREWER, Henry 1865 - 23
Oct 1938 B "Died at Peru,

FREWER (continued)
IN"
FRITZ, Rosemarie 1896 - 21
Aug 1970 - "Died at Cedar
Lake, IN"
FRITZER, Edger O 1885 - 26
Feb 1947 B
Bertha 183 - 13ct 1958 B
FRITZER, Charles 1874 - 9
July 1940 C
FUREY, Ellen 1854 - 13 Mar
1943 A
Julia 1880 - 3 May 1945 A
FUTA, Anna 1874 - 13 Aug
1948 E
GACKI, Felix 1875 - 1937 G
Jennie 1880 - 22 Aug 1970
G (Nee: Kurek)
GACKI, Lillian 1899 - 1970
D
Stephen 1884 - 1932 D
GADACZ, Joanna 1883 sister
- 1905
Wojciech   1845   father -
1884 D
GAFFNEY, Wm J 1901 - 12
Aug 1967 C
GALLAGHER, Rev Joseph
1869 - 19 Aug 1946 Com-
munity Cemetery ND
GALLAGHER, Rev Hugh
1873 - 12 Dec 1949 Com-
munity Cemetery ND
GALLAS, Stanley 1868 - 16
Aug 1957 C
Pearl 1869 - 1920 C
Martin 19 Oct 1905 - 4 Mar
1979 C
GALAZKIEWICZ,   Frances
1862 - 30 Aug 1943 F
John 1856 - 1915 F
GANG, Florian 1865 - 28 Oct
1941 A
GANTERT, Carl F 1901 - 14
Feb 1968 D "Died at
Niles, MI"

GANTERT, Fred C 1903 - 23
July 1965 E
GAPCZYNSKI,   Jan   1921 -
1921 E
Jozef 1917 - 1921 E
Jadwiga 1885 mother - 1927
E (Nee: Niezgodski)
Klara 1916 - 1927 E
GAPSKI, Regina 1914 - 1936
F
Bertha 1890 - 27 Apr 1940
F (Nee: Budzinski)
Mary 1890 - 12 Mar 1966 F
Jacob 1887 - 1975 F
GAPSKI, Jozefa 1858 - 29
June 1947 F
Walenty 1856 father - 17
June 1939 F
Michalina 1892 - 1898 F
GARD, Mary 1873 - 7 May
1939 A
GARNER, Mary 1868 - 13
June 1950 C
GARY, Elaine 1925 - 1974 F
Casimir 1915 - 19-- F
infant no date - 18 Oct 1956
F (Joseph J & Pauline G
Laskowski same lot)
GASSENSMITH,   Raymond
1891 - 23 Nov 1970 -
GAY, Dean Norman R 1919 -
31 Oct 1966 E
GAYLIS, F 1878 - 26 Aug
1953 -
GEABLER, Walter F 1879 -
1954 C
Mary M 1882 - 1974 C
(Joseph & Julia K Cza-
nowski same lot)
GEABLER, G 1880 - 6 Jan
1954 C
GEABLER, Blanche 1876 - 8
Mar 1942 D
GEABLER, John S 1871 - 11
Nov 1942 F
Lottie 1877 - 2 May 1941 F

GEABLER (continued)
(Nee: Poczekaj)
GEIDEO, J 1881 - 27 Aug
1956 D "Died at Elkhart,
IN"
GEHRING, John J 1861 - 16
Oct 1943 D
Louise 1888 - 12 May 1958
D
GEMBARZEWSKI, Joseph 3
Mar 1897 - 31 Mar 1942 D
"IN Pvt 69 Fld Arty 95 Div
WWI"
Hattie 1890 - 6 Sept 1980 D
(Nee: Sechowski)
Katharine 1859 - 22   Mar
1939 D
George 1853 - 1931 D
GERCHER, Melanie no date
- 11 June 1962 A
GERENCHER, Vera 1867 -
15 Oct 1938 G
GERGACZ, John J no date -
23 June 1948 A
Elizabeth 1872 - 23 Apr
1939 A
GERGACZ, Wm 1897 - 14
Jan 1955 B
Javos 1873 - 1929 B
Katalin 1875 - 1922 B
Rosilean 1898 - 1921 B
GIAZELLA, George 1889 -
25 Jan 1960 C
GIBBONS, M 1871 - 25 Mar
1957 C
GIELUPIC, no name 1901 -
17 Oct 1955 B
GIERSZ, Walentyna 1886 -
1915 C (Jozef & Magda-
lina Gruszynski same lot)
GIERSZ, Genowefa 1896 -
1900 C
Walerya 1909 - 1916 C
Klara 1897 - 1919 C
Teodor 1904 - 1932 C
Frank 1871 - 18 July 1941

GIERSZ (continued)
C
Sophie 1876 - 8 Nov 1949 C
GEIRSZ, Jakob 1840 - 1916
A
Helen 1843 - 1923 A (Jo-
sephine Leonard same lot)
GIERZYNSKI, Stella 1880
mother - 1928 E
Joseph Leo 1878 father - 3
Feb 1939 E
GILLEN, Frank 1883 - 4 Jan
1966 -
GILROY, Louise 1886 - 28
Nov 1961 B
GINTER, Anna 1873 - 1899 C
(Boleslaw, Wanda, Clara
B, & Antonina Ginter
Luzny same lot)
GISH, Stephen K 1886 - 1939
E (Lawrence Sowala;
Richard Daniel Cook; &
Ladyslaw & Mary Kruk
same lot)
GLOST, Dennis 1946 - 21
June 1960 E
GNOTH, William 1898 - 9
Mar 1959 A
Wm H 1896 - 1920 A
Ellen I 1893 - 6 Aug 1969 A
Michael J 1893 - 19-- A
Anna M 1899 - 19-- A
(Matthew & Anna Grabow-
ski same lot)
GNOTH, Valentine Aug 1864
father - 1924 C
Elizabeth 1861 mother - 7
July 1940 C (Nee: Mul-
ner)
Martin 1884 - 1921 C
Joseph 1888 - 1923 C
Mary 1890 - 1920 C
Mary 1888 - 14 Dec 1942 C
(Nee: Tobalski) "Wife of
Martin Gnoth"
GNOTH, Louis M no date - 8

GNOTH (continued)
June 1943 -
GOEPFRICH, Robert no date
- 20 Jan 1946 D
GOEPFRICH, Rose 1906 - 6
Dec 1947 C
GOEPFRICH, George 1865 -
22 June 1942 C
GOHEEN, Gertrude 1888 - 23
July 1971 -
GOLABOWSKI, Antonina 14
June 1857 mother - 14 Mar
1930 D
Michael 12 Sept 1852 father
- 1934 D
Roman F Sr 18 July 1881 -
7 Oct 1972 D
Helena A 24 Apr 1883 sister
- 28 Mar 1896 D
GOLATA, Michael 1841 fa-
ther - 1891 D
Karolina 1845 mother -
1923 D
GOLUBSKI, Antony Oct 1854
- 22 Oct 1911 C
GONDECK, Henry no date -
29 Sept 1942 C
Josephine 1887 - 15 Sept
1973 C
Maryann 1878 - 4 Aug 1950
C
GONDECK, Frank 1862 father
1929 G
Mary M 1849 mother - 1910
G (Nee: Robczynski)
Julius F 1895 brother -
1926 G
Frank J 1908 - 1978 G "Pvt
US Army"
GONSIOROWSKI, Jozefa
1819 - 1899 D
Frank 1846 father - 1925 D
Agnes 1857 mother - 1936
G (Nee: Krieger)
Helen Gonsiorowski Tur-
zynski 1874 - 1897 D

GONSIOROWSKI (continued)
"Wife of Joseph"
GONSIOROWSKI, Elge D
1912 - 1937 C (Nee:
Laskowicz) "Wife of Hil-
ary C Gonsiorowski"
(Jozefa Pieniazkiewicz
same lot)
GONSIOROWSKI, Marya 1873
- 20 Feb 1949 C
Sylvester 1893 - 10 Oct
1952 C
Hilary C 1908 - 9 Feb 1953
C (Joseph D Pie-
niaszkiewicz same lot)
GONSIOROWSKI, Rose 1887
mother - 1 Apr 1962 C
(Jacob & Maryanna Sta-
siak same lot)
GONSIOROWSKI, Sylvester
1881 - 10 Sept 1959 F
Irene Marie 1913 - 1930 F
(Leonard & Antony Las-
kowski same lot)
GONZEN, E 1888 - 22 Aug
1954 A
GOOLEY, V 1870 - 12 Jan
1955 B
GOOZDANOWICH, L 1883 -
7 June 1954 G
GORACZEWSKI, Walery 5
Apr 1820 - 20 Oct 1895 F
GORBITZ, Michael 1862 -
1919 C
Michael F 1888 - 1940 C
Lena 1892 - 1968 C
GORDY, Charles 1891 - 18
Oct 1961 C
GORKA, Waclaw 1879 father
- 21 Nov 1944 A
Emilia 1881 mother - 1918
A
Veronica 1907 daughter - 22
Dec 1956 A
William 1850 - 17 Aug
1942 A

20

GORKA, Frank J 1880 - 27 Aug 1959 H
Joanna F 1881 - 21 June 1952 H (Nee: Hosinski)
GORKA, Katarzyna 1859 mother - 1925 C (Nee: Skoniecki)
Mary 1885 mother - 13 Aug 1963 C (Nee: Hosinski)
Franciszek 1855 father - 1894 C
Mary 1882 - 14 Dec 1962 C (Nee: Kreczmer)
GORKA, Anna 1899 - 1907 E
Klementyna 1904 - 1904 E
Konstancia 1860 mother - 1926 E (Nee: Buzalski)
Wincenty 1854 father - 1922 E
GORNIEWICZ, Mary 1880 - 24 Feb 1953 F
Carl 1879 - 12 Apr 1954 F
GORSKI, Irvin F 1917 - 1918 C
Marie 1914 - no date C
Marie J 1906 - 1907 C
Irvin 1921 Son - 21 June 1939 C
Victoria 1877 mother - 1934 C (Nee: Otolski)
Marion 1874 father - 1924 C
GORSKI, Edmund 1882 - 21 Feb 1969 F
Josephine 1883 - 18 Apr 1945 F
Margaret 1914 - 19-- F
GORSKI, Marion 1867 - 25 Sept 1898 C
GOULD, Emma 2 hours old - 26 Nov 1971 -
GOUR, Phillias D 1872 - 11 Apr 1938 B
GRABARZ, Wincenty no date - 25 Sept 1898 F
GRABARZ, Anna 1867 - 5 Mar 1947 F (Nee: Golata)

GRABARZ (continued)
Andrzej 1863 - 1934 F
George 1879 - 18 Sept 1967 F
GRABARZ, Angela 4 June 1892 - 25 Feb 1910 G
Frances 1889 - 1932 G
Ralph 1903 - 1955 G
Helen 1887 - 1907 G
no name 1865 mother - 1939 G
no name 1859 father - 1904 G
GRABOWSKI, Anna 18 Dec 1846 wife - 4 Apr 1890 A
Matthew 10 Feb 1848 - 14 Feb 1898 A (William & Ellen Gnoth; & Michael J & Anna M Gnoth same lot)
GRABOWSKI, Ferdinand 1873 - 1908 C
Sophie 1875 - 24 Feb 1948 C (Nee: Ober) (Antony, Edward, Victor, & Mary Ober same lot)
GRACZOL, John Steven 1869 - 16 June 1951 E
Agnes 1869 - 7 Aug 1957 E (Helen, Franciszek, Wladyslaw, & Walter Woznicki same lot)
GRAF, Frank 1910 - 18 May 1968 A
Esther 1886 - 17 Jan 1960 A
Frank 1882 - 24 Dec 1958 A
GRAJKOWSKI, Mary 1865 - 1931 G
Antonette 1894 - 10 Aug 1965 G
Martin 1859 - 1919 G
Theodore 1908 - 1924 G
Stanley 1888 - 5 Aug 1972 G
GRAMLE, Julius 1907 - 16 June 1948 -

GRAMS, Marcyanna 1 Jan 1864 grandmother - 22 Oct 1894 D "Wife of Jan Grams; nee: Kareszewski)

GRAMS, Joanna no date - 17 Sept 1894 D "Our mother, wife of Patrich Grams"
Max J Sr 1895 - 18 Nov 1963 D
Josephine B -no dates- D

GRAMZA, Luke J -no dates- A
Julia 1887 - 11 Nov 1956 A

GRAMZA, Rose 1880 mother - 12 Nov 1966 D (Nee: Wozniak)
Edward 1877 - 1927 D (Julia Szewczyk same lot)

GRAMZA, Josephine 1880 - 7 Sept 1960 F (Nee: Egierski)
Frances Aug 1874 - 6 May 1922 F
Leo R Gramze 1906 husband - 1937 F

GRANT, Frederich F 26 May 1911 son - 22 Nov 1976 A (Josephine, Frances, & Frank Grontkowski same lot)

GRAU, Margaret 1866 - 1 Mar 1939 F

GREENE, Mary 1882 - 18 May 1948 C

GREGA, Paul 1865 - 1937 D
Anna 1875 - 1935 D (Eleanor Superczynski same lot)

GREIF, John A 1878 - 9 Apr 1953 F

GRIESHABER, Wilhelmina 1876 - 3 Feb 1939 D

GRIMM, Barbara 1848 - 5 Jan 1939 F

GRINMAN, Julianna 1885 - 11 Oct 1960 C

GRINMAN (continued)
Mary 1885 - 3 Dec 1969 C

GROCHOWSKI, Stanley 1888 - 5 Aug 1972 G
Antonina 1891 - 10 Aug 1965 G
John 1891 - 16 Sept 1961 G

GROFF, M ? - 7 June 1955 B

GRONTKOWSKI, Clara 1886 - 1911 C
Karol 1847 father - 1923 C
Anna 6 July 1853 mother - 21 Apr 1936 C (Nee: Wentland)

GRONTKOWSKI, John C 1875 - 25 Apr 1955 C
Mary A 1879 - 22 Sept 1961 C (Nee: Kubiak)
Florens no dates C
Edmund no dates C
Irene no dates C
Louis no dates C
Edward no dates C

GRONTKOWSKI, Josephine 10 Oct 1910 - 21 Oct 1914 A
Frances 8 Feb 1879 mother - 22 Feb 1940 A (Nee: Gish)
Frank 24 Mar 1877 father - 28 June 1941 A (Frederich F Grant same lot)

GRUBER, Mary 1896 - 31 Aug 1972 -

GRUBER, Andrew 1866 - 14 June 1941 A

GRUGAN, Thomas J 1870 - 16 June 1943 A

GRUSE, Frances 1889 - 6 July 1969 E

GRUSZYNSKI, Jozef 1855 father - 1924 C
Magdalena 1864 mother - 1906 C (Walentyna Giersz same lot)

GRZEGOREK, Leokadya 8

GRZEGOREK (continued)
Sept 1882 - 6 Sept 1903 F
(Alex Luzny same lot)
GRZELAK, Konstanty 1885 -
1916 A "Married Mary
Jankowski"
Stanislaw 1914 - 1915 A
GRZESK, Mary 1865 - 4 May
1943 C (Nee: Kazmierski)
Julian L 1867 - 10 March
1942 C
Andrzej 1840 - 1934 C
Katarzyna 1843 - 1896 C
GRZESK, Ladislaw 1863
father - 1935 D
Agnes 1865 mother - 1937
D (Nee: Konczan)
Henry J 1891 - 1920 D
Stephania 1894 - 29 May
1966 D
GRZESK, Tomasz 1849 -
1926 C
Antonina 1857 - 1906 C
(Nee: Strantz)
GRZEZINSKI, Elizabeth 1898
- 29 Sept 1960 C
Frank 1904 - 25 Nov 1966 C
Vivian 1927 - 1930 C
Jozef 26 Aug 1860 father -
8 Aug 1920 C
Anna 24 June 1877 - 21 Mar
1931 C (Nee: Rusiewicz)
GUDAJTYS, Maryanna 1869
mother 1931 C
Wincenty 1860 father 1930
C
GUILEFOYLE, John D ? - 11
Feb 1969 - "Died at Mi-
chigan City, IN"
GUILEFOYLE, Mary E 1873
- 12 Sept 1944 A
GUILEFOYLE, David 1865 -
27 Sept 1945 B
GUIZYNSKI, Joseph Leo ? -
3 Feb 1939 E
GUNDECK, Leon 1863 father

GUNDECK (continued)
- 1929 C
Agnes 1880 mother 1910 C
(Nee: Jenczak)
Veronica 1872 mother -
1899 C (Nee: Krzeszew-
ski)
Joseph -no dates- C
Stanley -no dates- C
GUNDECK, John Feb 1899 -
1900 C
Peter 1867 father - 1931 C
Maryann 1877 mother -
1931 C
John 1830 father - 1921 C
Mary 1842 mother - 1908 C
(Nee: Kush)
Josephine -no dates- C
Andrew -no dates- C
John -no dates- C
Lottie -no dates- C
GURDA, Marya 17 Dec 1873
- 20 July 1905 E (Nee:
Kowalski)
GUTHRIE, Flora 1868 - 7
Aug 1948 A
GUZICKI, John baby - June
1952 A
Helen 1890 - 1927 A "Wife
of Stanley Guzicki" (Paul
P, Pauline, Roman, &
Hattie Luzny same lot)
GYOLCS, Veronica 1890 - 29
Aug 1940 -
HAAS, A E 1885 - 20 Feb
1941 A
HACK, Josephine A Collner
1923 - 28 Jan 1965 E
HADRICK, John Sr 1880 - 24
Feb 1953 C
HADRICK, Clara 1900 - 6
Sept 1945 C
HAFNER, Anna 1885 - 1 Feb
1972 -
HAGER, George 1896 - 8
Mar 1943 E

HAGERTY, Julia 1877 - 14 Feb 1947 A
Bridget 1858 - 4 June 1943 A
HAHAN, Joyce 1930 - 14 May 1971 -
HAJDU, Vendele 1882 - 24 Feb 1942 A
HAJDUCKI, Anna Kurek 1877 - 23 July 1954 A (Joseph J Kurek same lot)
HAJDUCKI, George J 1878 - 22 Nov 1948 C
Ignacy 1843 - no date C
Katarzyna -no dates- C
Alex -no dates- C
HALL, Josephine Barbara 1883 - 6 Dec 1950 B
Ray 1885 - 4 Sept 1969 B
HAMMER, Loretta 1892 - 10 July 1958 D
Fred 1892 - 22 Dec 1957 D
HAMMES, Dorothy 1904 - 17 Jan 1965 B "Died at Kankakee, IL"
HANEY, Helen 1906 - 9 Sept 1970 -
Thelma 1901 - 14 Jan 1973 -
HANEY, L 1870 - 19 July 1954 A
HANEY, Charles E 1887 - 6 May 1948 C
HANEY, Harold 1897 - 4 Dec 1951 F
HANKEY, Frank W 1868 - 30 Oct 1948 C
HANLEY, Margaret 1876 - 8 Sept 1943 A "Died at Chicago, IL"
HANS, Caroline 1864 - 21 July 1940 A
HANYZEWSKI, John 1869 - 24 Sept 1947 E (J Nagy same lot)
HANYZEWSKI, John 1919 -

HANYZEWSKI (continued) 9 Feb 1962 F
HANYZEWSKI, Michael 1864 - 1 Feb 1899 -
HARDIN, Rose 1906 - 10 Feb 1948 C
HARMACINSKI, Franciszka 9 Oct 1879 - 21 May 1917 E (Nee: Szynski)
Wawrzyn 1862 - 12 July 1940 E
HARRIGAN, Cornelius 1883 - 20 Feb 1949 C
HARRIS, Frank 1894 - 15 Sept 1963 C
HARSANYI, Paul 1902 - 3 June 1968 B
Anna Theresa 1898 - 12 Dec 1971 B
HART, Rev Joseph 1892 - 28 Sept 1946 Community Cemetery ND
HARTUCH, Mary 1893 - 14 Aug 1957 C
HARTWICK, Jacob 1893 - 23 Sept 1945 C
HARTWICK, Sylvester A 1918 - 19 Aug 1966 C
HAZINSKI, Estera 1945 - 24 Oct 1945 D
Lottie 1886 mother - 1979 D (Nee: Grzesk)
Alexander S 1888 father - 1927 D
Helen 1890 - no date D
HAZINSKI, Ollie J 1904 - 1980 D "Pvt US Army WWII"
George L 1873 - 5 Dec 1926 D
Josephine 25 Oct 1872 - 6 July 1955 D (Nee: Kaczmarek)
Norma Jean 1931 - 1932 D
HAZINSKI, Martha 1884 - 11 Dec 1957 E (Nee: Kowa-

HAZINSKI (continued)
lek)
Joseph ? 30 Apr 1942 E
HEIDER, Edward 1881 - 27
Mar 1949 Community
Cemetery ND
HEIL, Margaret 1865 - 27
Aug 1941 D
HEINRICKS, A 1881 - 16 Oct
1956 B
HEINTSKILL, Rev Andrew
1913 - 24 Oct 1946 Com-
munity Cemetery ND
HEISER, Nell 1852 - 12 Sept
1962 B
Clarence 1875 - 5 Feb 1946
B
HELMINIAK, Frank 1881 -
23 May 1946 C
HEPLER, Mary 1859 - 27
Feb 1953 B
HEPLER, George 1857 - 14
Dec 1940 B
HERTHOGE, M 1868 - 8
July 1953 E
Theofil 1869 - 18 Feb 1950
E
HESS, Timothy 10 days old -
12 Jan 1947 A
HESTON, Alonzo 1881 - 19
Feb 1942 B
HESTON, Eleanor J 1885 - 2
Feb 1973 - "Died at Tu-
lane, CA"
HIGHBARGER, John S 1940
- 11 Aug 1973 - "Died at
Hyde Park, NY"
HIMBER, Frank 1888 - 29
Dec 1951 C
Anna 1880 - 26 Nov 1947 C
HIMES, Virginia M 1936 - 7
Mar 1970 -
HIRL, Joseph 1877 - 5 Dec
1942 F
HISER, M 1881 - 17 Oct
1956 -

HISHON, C 1888 - 30 Jan
1961 D
HISS, Beatrice 1891 - 19 Dec
1966 B
John 1883 - 3 Aug 1947 B
HOBAN, Maurice 1881 - 9
Apr 1960 D
HODOSY, William 1901 - 11
Dec 1964 D
HOFFER, Charles J 1924 -
1948 C
Piroska 1862 - 12 May 1939
C
HOFFMAN, Gertrude 1882 -
14 Feb 1966 C
HOGAN, William 1891 - 7
Jan 1965 D
HOJNACKI, Salomea 1 Apr
1883 - 30 Aug 1945 A
"Wife of Walter Hojnacki,
nee: Wawrzon" (Stella &
John Wawrzon same lot)
HOLCOMB, Edward 1887 -
29 Jan 1966 E
HOLEWINSKI, Josefa 1869
mother - 25 Oct 1943 E
Walenty 1863 - 1936 E
John W no date - 7 Feb
1931 E "IN Pvt 5 Eng 7
Div"
Bertha J Merrick 5 Apr 1898
- 18 Dec 1978 E (Nee:
Mazukiewicz)
HOLEWINSKI, Frank J 1896
- 1923 E
Frank 1875 husband - 1931
E
Mary 1881 wife - 1968 E
HOLLAND, Margaret 1864 -
8 Sept 1958 E
HOOVER, Glen 1896 - 12
Dec 1969 no grave site
HORKA, Antony 8 May 1878
- 21 Aug 1898 C
Stanislaus 1827 - 1909 C
Mary 1839 - 1895 C

HORKA (continued)
Clara 1905 - 1926 C
Joseph 1863 - 1928 C
HORKOWSKI, Cecelia 1885 - 29 Mar 1960 C
HORVATH, Robert 1 month old - 10 Aug 1941 A
HORVATH, John 1877 - 12 Dec 1961 A
HORVATH, Steve 1908 - 27 Mar 1959 A
HORVATH, John 1886 - 2 Aug 1944 C "Died at Laporte, IN"
HORVATH, Lydia 1873 - 25 Dec 1959 C
Irene 1919 - 10 Nov 1958 C
HORVATH, Stephen S 1875 - 15 June 1950 C
HORVATH, L 1870 - 16 Oct 1966 C
Mary no date - 17 July 1940 C
HORVATH, Elizabeth 1887 - 30 Oct 1966 C
Anna no date - 5 June 1963 C
HORVATH, Theresa 1883 - 19 Nov 1963 D
HORVATH, Elizabeth 1907 - 19 Oct 1957 D
Michael 1900 - 4 Dec 1961 D
HORVATH, Bertha 9 days old - 16 Oct 1966 G
HORVATH, Anton 1879 - 10 Feb 1951 H
HORVATH, Theresa 1866 - 16 Dec 1968 -
HOSINSKI, Helen 1905 - 1905 A (Joseph Janowiak; Wm & Michael North; Michael Baloun; & Joseph Wcisel same lot)
HOSINSKI, Nikodem F 13 May 1878 - 7 Oct 1930 A

HOSINSKI (continued)
Apolonia 21 Jan 1883 - 7 Nov 1970 A (Nee: Egierski) "Died at Universal Park, MD"
Antony W 27 Mar 1910 - 7 June 1924 A (Magdelena Kowalski same lot)
HOSINSKI, John I 1870 - 1908 A
Helen 1873 - 26 Sept 1942 A (Nee: Kizer)
Robert C 1899 - 30 June 1938 A
HOSINSKI, Jadwiga M 1883 - 28 June 1971 B (Nee: Grzesk) "Died at Houston, TX"
Joseph B 1881 - 1926 B
HOSINSKI, Ignac no date - 17 Apr 1888 C
Marya 1855 wife - 24 Oct 1921 C (Nee: Pierzynski)
Ignacy 1882 - 25 Mar 1951 C
Marta 1877 - 12 Nov 1955 C
HOSINSKI, Magdalena 1809 mother - 1902 D
Antoni F 1850 father - 1928 D
Rozalie B 1857 mother - 1928 D (Nee: Kowalski)
Zofia 7 Jan 1892 - 3 Sept 1892 D
Teresa 1893 - 1894 D
HOSINSKI, Antonina 1819 - 10 Jan 1875 D (Nee: Kowalski) "First wife of Ignac Hosinski" (Anton & Elizabeth Latosinski same lot)
HOSINSKI, Rev Sylvester 1885 - 27 Aug 1953 D "Ordained 25 June 1913"
Rozalia 1846 - 29 Dec 1932 D (Nee: Kujawa)

HOSINSKI (continued)
Frank 1836 - 30 Jan 1918 D
Edwina R 26 Aug 1907 - 26
Mar 1908 D
HOSINSKI, Louise 1878 - 21
July 1939 F
W 1 day old - 1920 F
Helen 1907 - 1910 F
Joseph 1917 - 1918 F
Albin 1911 - 1924 F
Antony 1880 - 29 Apr 1967
F
HOULIHAN, Rev E J 1875 -
16 Aug 1940 A
HOWARD, Leona 1906 - 6
June 1973 -
HOWARD, Genevieve 1871 -
17 Jan 1939 B
HOWLETT, no name 1869 -
1 May 1948 D
HUBBARD, L 1881 - 13 Jan
1954 C
HUBER, John A 1883 - 12
Dec 1945 A
Edward 1873 - 24 Nov 1944
A
HUDAK, Walter 1896 - 1919
E
Pawel 1 Jan 1858 - 6 Feb
1902 E
Katharine 1882 - 19 Sept
1960 E
HUDSON, Nellie A 1863 - 7
Feb 1949 F
HUDSON, Elizabeth 1873 - 8
Dec 1941 D
John 1912 - 20 June 1940 D
HUDZINSKI, Frank no dates
D
HUGHES, Jon Daniel 5
months old - 26 Nov 1968
-
HUGHES, Joseph 1861 - 1
Apr 1946 A "Died in Cas-
sapolis, MI"
HUKY, C 1890 - 22 Mar 1957

HUKY (continued)
C
HUMBERGER, Martha 1885
- 25 Mar 1971 C
Adolph 1883 - 11 Dec 1957
C
HUMES, Stella 1870 - 30
Jan 1943 D
HUMPHREY, I 1870 - 9
May 1954 A
HUMPHREY, Lena 1867 -
10 May 1951 C
ILLES, Venczel F 1879 - 25
July 1965 F
IVANCSICS, Frank 1856 - 12
Jan 1942 C
IVANCSICS, Agnes 1895 - 11
Feb 1973 F
Nikoles 1894 - 1 Dec 1938
F
IVANKOVICS, Joseph 1881 -
20 Apr 1967 C
E 1883 - 13 Jan 1954 C
IVANKOVICS, Rose 1894 - 8
Jan 1939 H
John 1884 - 9 Aug 1966 H
IWANOWSKI, Peter ? - 9
Oct 1900 E
IWINSKI, Maryanna 14 Dec
1873 - 31 Jan 1902 C
(Nee: Rozplochowski)
IZDEPSKI, Franciszek 1844
- 1913 H
Anna 1844 - no date H
(Nee: Kalewicz)
JABLONSKI, Clem J ? -
1937 D "IN Pvt 532 Aero
Sq"
no name 1856 father - 1915
D
Jozef -no dates- D
Stanislaw -no dates- D
Pelegia -no dates- D
Wiktorya 1883 mother -
1905 D
JACKOWIAK, Victoria 16

JACKOWIAK (continued)
Oct 1890 - 8 Sept 1959 D
(Nee: Gettke)
Stanley 24 Apr 1882 - 2 Feb
1957 D
Adam -no dates- D
Anna 7 May 1911 - 30 Aug
1920 D
Zymund -no dates- D
JACOBSEN, Jennie 1888 - 23
Jan 1940 C "Died at New
York City, NY"
JAGODZINSKI, Stanislaw -no
dates- brother C (Wlady-
slaw & Ludwika Korno-
wicz same lot)
JAKUBOWICZ, A 1887 - 16
Dec 1939 -
JAKUBOWICZ, Nicodemus
1885 - 1932 C
Ignacy 1852 father - 26 Oct
1938 C
Anna 1857 mother - 1925 C
Hedwige 1902 - 1902 C
Peter P 19 Apr 1898 - 17
May 1944 C
JANICKI, Dennis ? - 19 Jan
1940 C
JANIK, Clara 4 July 1897
wife - 15 Apr 1929 A
JANISZEWSKI, Rozalia 1882
mother - 2 Mar 1941 C
JANKOWIAK, Antony 1899 -
3 July 1945 A
Walter J 6 Apr 1896 - 26
Sept 1950 "IN Pvt 115 Inf
29 Div WWI" A
Agnes -no dates- A
Boleslaw 1889 - 1916 A
Mieczyslaw 1909 - 1909 A
Thomas 1856 - 24 June
1939 A
Frances 1859 - 4 Jan 1943
A (Nee: Kalolinski)
JANKOWSKI, Konstanty 1856
- 1926 G

JANKOWSKI, S -no dates- C
Agnes Horvath 1860 - 19
Mar 1939 C
JANOWIAK, Jacob 1848 fa-
ther - 1928 A
Helen 1853 mother - 1912 A
(Nee: Mnichowski)
Leo 1885 - 1901 A
Joseph 1890 - 1899 A (Wm
& Michael North; Michael
Baloun; J Wcisel; & Helen
Hosinski same lot)
JANOWIAK, Tadeusa 1911 -
1920 B
Esther 1908 - 8 June 1951
B
Antony 1878 father - 2 Sept
1955 B
Josephine M 1887 - 3 Sept
1956 (Nee: Kujawski) B
(no name Makielski; John
& Josephine Saberniak; &
Michael Rutowski same
lot)
JANOWIAK, Stanley S 1880 -
25 Nov 1940 D
Jennie (Joanna) 1887 - 12
Mar 1942 D (Nee: Wituc-
ki)
JANOWIAK, Szymon 1855
grandfather - 10 Mar 1930
D
Franciszka 1861 grand-
mother - 1936 D (Nee:
Torzewski)
JANOWSKI, Teofil 5 Sept
1864 - 24 May 1954 C
Barbara 15 June 1879 - 4
Jan 1925 C (Nee: Roytek)
JANOWSKI, Teofil ? - 14
Oct 1916 D
Mary 1865 - 22 Apr 1940 D
(Nee: Stypczynski)
JANOWSKI, Ann Therese
1928 daughter - 20 Aug
1946 F

JANOWSKI (continued)
Vern J 1894 husband, father
- 1936 F
Adeline M 1900 - 21 Nov
1965 "Died at Petoskey,
MI" F
JANOWSKI, Veronica 1906 -
1978 D
Zofia 1892 - 1903 D
Frank 1859 - 25 Feb 1941 D
Maryann 1816 - 1894 D
Martin 1829 - 1908 D
Wladyslawa -no dates- D
Alojzy -no dates- D
Stanislaw -no dates- D
Franciszek -no dates- D
Julia A 1870 - 24 Apr 1951
D (Nee: Jankowski)
JANOWSKI, Joanna 8 July
1886 - 11 Jan 1906 F
Michael 19 Oct 1852 - 3
Nov 1913 F
Leokadya 1880 mother -
1919 F (Nee: Chmielew-
ski)
Mieczyslaw 1879 - 31 Mar
1939 F (Joseph V Rayski
& Michael Kolupa same
lot)
JANSO, Cecelia 1872 - 29
July 1963 C
Ernest J 1894 - 22 Dec
1968 C
JARLATH, B 1903 - 2 Nov
1949 Community Cemetery
ND
JAROSZEWSKI, Maryanna 8
Dec 1827 - 30 July 1900 F
Tomasz 21 Dec 1821 - 25
Dec 1895 F
JASICKI, John 1877 father -
13 Nov 1940 E
Stella 1880 - 25 Sept 1960
E
JASKOWIAK, Stanley 1862 -
9 July 1947 A

JASKOWIAK (continued)
Frances 1868 - 25 Apr 1961
A
Blase 1898 - 8 Apr 1951 A
(James Lukaszewski same
lot)
JAWORSKI, Pelagia 1894 -
1920 E
Jan 1860 father - 19 Apr
1932 E
Maryanna 1868 mother - 17
Apr 1947 E (Nee: An-
drzejewski) (Wawrzyn &
Jadwiga Andrzejewski
same lot)
JAWORSKI, Boleslaw 1841
father - 18 July 1883 C
Josephine Zambrzny 8 Dec
1856 - 17 Apr 1898 C
JEGIER, John 1860 father -
15 June 1903 E (Note:
tombstone reads 1904)
"Wife Katharine interred
St Joseph Polish Ceme-
tery"
John S 29 Aug 1891 - 6 July
1966 E "IN Pvt Co A 36
Inf WWI"
JESSIAK, James 6 Feb 1884
husband - 3 Jan 1933 F
Hattie wife -no dates- F
(Nee: Dobrzykowski)
JOHNSTON, Barbara 1903 -
29 July 1939 F "Died at
Buchanan, MI"
Margaret 1903 - 29 July
1939 F
JONES, Herbert E 1903 - 6
Mar 1969 D
John ? - 10 Aug 1949 D
JOYCE, R 1864 - 9 Dec 1954
D (Died at Colorado
Springs, CO)
JOYCE, Marie F 1898 - 21
July 1967 A
JUREK, Andrzej 1849 - 1904

JUREK (continued)
C
Agnieszka 1853 - 1936 C
Jan 1881 - 1904 C
Walenty 1889 - 1922 C
Adam 1907 - 1907 C
JUSZCZAK, Franciszka 1886
- 1938 F
Josef 1885 - 18 Dec 1938 F
"Placowka #125 - Polish
soldier)
KACZMAREK, Vincent 1856
- 1924 C
Mary 1856 wife - 1936 C
Magdalen 1892 - 1907 C
Stanly 1901 - 5 Jan 1945 C
KACZMAREK, Joseph 1885
- 26 May 1938 D "IN Pvt
323 Fld Arty 83rd Div"
J 1882 - 18 Sept 1955 D
Frances 1886 - 16 Feb 1952
D
KACZMAREK, Marcin 29
June 1856 - 14 Dec 1936 -
KACZMAREK, Jozef 1882
father - 25 July 1908 D
(Gyorgy & Rose Torok
same lot)
KACZMAREK, Waclaw 1878
- 1919 E
KALAMAJA, Anna 22 July
1839 - 14 Jan 1901 F (Jo-
seph Bartoszek Jr same
lot)
KALAMAJSKI, Mary mother
-no dates- C
Leonard father -no dates- C
Anna grandmother -no
dates- C "Wife of Alex
Kalamajski"
KALAMAJSKI, Tony 1881 -
13 May 1955 D
Bessie 1884 - 19-- D (Nee:
Hathaway)
Alexander 1881 - 11 July
1959 D

KALAMAJSKI (continued)
Helen (Lena) 1882 - 8 Dec
1963 D (Nee: Grosch)
KALAMAJSKI, Sophie J 1891
- 25 Sept 1961 D
Lottie 1875 - 21 June 1960
D
KALCZYNSKI, Jan 1875 -
1915 A
Franciszek 1881 - 1917 A
(Bruno, Sophie, & George
Luzny same lot)
KALCZYNSKI, Wojciech
1839 - 1930 D
Maryanna 1852 - 1887 D
Mary 1860 - 20 Oct 1940 D
KALCZYNSKI, no name 1845
father 1899 F
Leokadya Jurek 1851
mother 1907 F (Alex &
Nellie Marshall same lot)
KALICKI, Katarzyna -no
dates- E
KALLINGER, Ignace 1870 -
29 June 1943 C
KALMAN, Victoria -no
dates- C
Charles J Jr 1902 - 1946 C
Paul -no dates- C
Elizabeth -no dates- C
Charles -no dates- C
KALMAR, Clara 1896 - 1919
C
Louis J 1894 - 29 Apr 1956
C "Died at Kokomo, IN"
KALMAR, Steve 1880 - 9
June 1959 G
Elizabeth 1885 - 9 July
1962 G
KAMAN, Mary Rose 1911 -
1957 B
John 1871 - 10 Oct 1947 B
N 1907 - 27 Jan 1957 B
KAMINSKI, Nikodem 1857 -
7 Jan 1940 D
Victoria 1866 - 1914 D

KAMINSKI (continued)
(Nee: Pawlak)
KAMINSKI, Leo N 1895 - 24
July 1952 D "Died at Chi-
cago, IL"
KAMINSKI, M 1875 - 20
June 1953 E
Eliguis 1895 - 1898 E
(Franciszek & Pelegia
Ciesiolka same lot)
KAMM, Dr Bernard 1900 - 7
July 1967 H
KANE, Mayme A 1886 - 21
Mar 1970 -
KANE, Arthur C 1886 - 18
Feb 1965 C "Died at
Niles, MI"
KASZA, Mary W Sept 1876 -
1916 A (Nee: Stachowiak)
(Martin, Maryanna, & Rev
Antony Stachowiak same
lot)
KASZYNSKI, Bertha 1876 -
24 Mar 1912 A
KATONA, Margaret 1881 - 23
July 1958 A
KAUFFMAN, Ada 1883 - 3
Dec 1958 B
KAZMIERCZAK, Rose 1918
- 19-- A
KAZMIERCZAK, Josephine
1872 - 2 Dec 1943 C (Nee:
Krakowski)
Andrzej ? - 6 July 1920 C
C 1900 - 4 Aug 1955 C
KAZMIERCZAK, Ignatius
1871 - 24 May 1938 E
Tillie Rose 1878 - 8 Apr
1952 E
KAZMIRSKI, no name 1868
mother - 1932 D
KEANS, Rev M 1884 - 22
Nov 1946 Community
Cemetery ND "Died at
New Bedford, MA"
KEARNEY, John J 1900 - 7

KEARNEY (continued)
May 1968 C
KEARNEY, Thomas J 1885 -
14 Nov 1955 Community
Cemetery ND
KEDZIORSKI, Pawel 1817 -
1883 D
Katarzyna 1832 wife - 1915
D
KEDZIORSKI, Steve 1881 - 4
Nov 1964 G
KEHOE, John 1885 - 16 Feb
1955 D
KELLER, Mary 1886 - 14
Dec 1961 D
KELLY, William 1858 - 13
Oct 1942 A
Vera 1884 - 4 Jan 1971 A
"Died at Montorosa, CA"
KELLY, Paul K 1918 - 6 Apr
1950 Community Cemetery
ND "Died at San Isidore,
South America"
KELLY, Elizabeth 1863 - 11
Mar 1941 A
Frank W 1899 - 25 Sept
1967 A
KELLY, Martha 1885 - 30
Oct 1961 C
KELLY, M G 1896 - 20 Apr
1953 B
KELLY, Michael J 1879 - 16
May 1942 D
KENNA, Marcella 1882 - 28
Apr 1968 A
KERESTESI, Frank M 1886 -
6 Aug 1945 B
Frances 1889 - 18 June
1955 B
KERIN, Bert Gale 1872 - 28
June 1943 - "Died at Cass
Co, MI"
KERTES, Louis 1871 - 29
June 1943 C
KERTIS, Alex 1880 - 6 Sept
1957 A

31

KERTISZ, Paul 1864 - 7 Mar 1942 A
KESSICK, Katharine 1884 - 27 Mar 1939 F
KESZEI, Vincent 1888 - 3 Sept 1969 -
KEVIN, C 1954 - 18 Jan 1957 A
KIERAN, John S 1914 son - 1929 B
John J 7 Jan 1889 - 12 Jan 1981 B
Mary 3 Dec 1892 - 22 Sept 1978 B (Nee: Strantz) (Frances Strantz same lot)
KIERAN, Katharine 1879 mother - 18 Aug 1939 D
John F 1869 father - 1932 D
KIERAN, Andrew 15 Oct 1855 - 1 May 1921 E
KIESTER, C 1880 - 10 Nov 1954 F
KILLELEA, Anna 1878 - 15 Nov 1945 A
Rosalea 1902 - 1 Apr 1950 A
KILLELEA, Marie 1892 - 10 July 1955 B
KIMMEL, Stella 1887 - 14 Feb 1966 F (Nee: Niedbalski)
Casimir 1882 - 1935 F
KIMMEL, Fred Casimir -no dates- F
Agnes 1856 - 1917 F
KINOWSKI, Konstanty 1841 - 22 Mar 1890 D (Jacob Tobolski same lot)
KINTZ, John 1874 - 30 Jan 1964 C
Edith 1875 - 2 Mar 1964 C
KIPP, Margaret 1913 - 14 May 1943 B
KIRSITS, John 1877 - 4 Feb 1958 F
KISH, Joseph 1861 - 21 May

KISH (continued) 1942 D
Dr Frank 1891 - 20 Jan 1950 D
Anna 1871 - 1 May 1951 D
KITKOWSKI, Bert 20 Apr 1872 father - 1936 A
Frances 7 Mar 1871 mother - 26 Jan 1941 A (Nee: Boinski)
KITKOWSKI, Stanislaw -no dates- C "Married Catharine Kosinski"
Stanislaw 1905 - 1906 C
Jan 1910 - 1915 C
Leonard J 1897 - 24 Mar 1962 C
KITKOWSKI, Julius -no dates- F
Anna 1870 - no date F (Nee: Kush)
KLAER, Anna 1864 - 8 Mar 1939 C
KLADUSZ, Agnes 1902 - 1926 F "Wife of John Kladusz"
KLAJBOR, John S 1915 - 7 Feb 1969 -
KLAWINSKI, Leo W ? - 20 Jan 1929 C
Wladyslaw 1859 - 1933 C
Leokadya 1870 - 1923 C (Nee: Sweda)
Alicya -no dates- C
Bronislaw -no dates- C
Edward -no dates- C
Carrie 1900 - 1933 C
KLEBOSITS, Helen 1885 - 31 Aug 1959 C
KLEBUSITS, Bela 1875 - 19 June 1938 C
P 1882 - 3 Nov 1954 C
M 1884 - 6 Aug 1954 C
Louis 1889 - 11 July 1966 C
KLEIN, Margaret 1880 - 6

KLEIN (continued)
Feb 1960 D
Harry B ? - 13 Oct 1952 D
KLOSINSKI, Julian 1881 father - 1933 E
Josephine 1882 mother - 1977 E
KLUSZYNSKI, Sylvester M 1871 son - 28 Jan 1939 C
Magdaline 1840 mother - 1911 C
KLYSZ, Michael 1851 - 1899 C
Josephine 1861 - 12 Jan 1939 C (Nee: Drajus)
Matthew Walter 22 Aug 1897 - 25 May 1954 C "IN Cpl 66 Arty CAC WWI" (Andrew Drajus same lot)
KLYSZ, Clara 1888 - 1 Mar 1943 D
Leonard 1885 - 4 Jan 1951 D
KNACH, Josef F 1869 - 1896 F
Katarzyna 1834 - 1920 F
Mary 22 May 1878 - 11 July 1914 F
Jakob June 1822 - 25 Nov 1911 F
KNOWLES, Mary 1882 - 25 Nov 1967 F
John 1878 - 4 Mar 1939 F "Died at Chicago, IL"
KOBER, N J 1899 - 3 Feb 1958 C
KOCH, M 1896 - 12 Apr 1954 D
KOCHANOWSKI, Jadwiga 1887 mother - 1931 B
Bronislawa 1882 - 1938 B (Nee: Sypniewski)
Stanislaw 1882 father 1935 B
KOCHANOWSKI, Salomea Nov 1842 mother - 1933 D

KOCHANOWSKI (continued)
(Nee: Nawrocki)
Pawel 15 Mar 1853 father - 20 Dec 1949 D
Rozalia 1886 daughter 1891 D
KOCHENDORFER, Leo 1888 - 28 Nov 1968 H
Mildred 1889 - 8 July 1949 H
Robert 1937 - 21 Sept 1973 H
Mary 2 days old - 8 Sept 1940 H
KOCSIS, Hattie 1898 - 2 Sept 1965 D
Mary 1871 - 25 Oct 1941 D
Andrew 1874 - 16 Feb 1941 D
KOCSIS, Alex 1878 - 25 Dec 1959 A
KOCSIS, Joseph 1883 - 1 May 1958 D
KOCZAN, Michael 1889 - 24 June 1969 C
Mary 1917 - 1920 C
Genevieve 1912 - 1951 C
Minai 1856 father - 1925 C
Michael Jr 1915 - 1934 C "Son of Michael & Catharine Koczan"
Anna 1908 - 1935 C "Wife of Joseph Koczan"
KOCZOROWSKI, Helen 1900 - 2 Sept 1948 A
Clem P 1902 - 28 Oct 1942 A
Peter 1860 - 13 Apr 1917 A
Agnes 1863 - 12 Jan 1942 A (Nee: Budnik)
KOCZOROWSKI, Agnieszka ? mother - 30 Oct 1904 C "Wife of Mike Koczorowski, nee: Tomaszewski"
KOEHLER, Estelle ? - 25 June 1973 D

33

KOEHLER (continued)
Lena 1882 - 8 Dec 1963 D
A 1882 - 13 May 1955 D
Alex 1881 - 11 July 1959 D
"Died at Chicago, IL"
KOLBER, Elizabeth 1871 -
24 Nov 1944 A
KOLCZYNSKI, Maryann 1860
- 1940 D
Stanislaw 1824 father -
1902 D
Anna 1826 mother - 1904 D
(Lillian Thilman same lot)
KOLCZYNSKI, Eleanor 1868
- 1947 A (Felix & Theresa
Przygocki; & Katarzyna
Rychlewski same lot)
KOLENDORFER, Katharyn
1873 - 24 Jan 1944 C
KOLENDORFER, Joseph
1871 - 27 Apr 1959 D
KOLESIAK, Stanislaus 7 July
1876 - 1934 A
Mary 18 June 1879 - 27 Dec
1967 A (Nee: Torzewski)
Jennie 1908 - 7 Dec 1947 A
KOLLER, Lillian 1939 - 15
Mar 1940 C
KOLLER, Margaret A 1898 -
2 Mar 1965 E
J 1899 - 26 Mar 1955 E
KOLOSAR, George 1881 - 19
May 1963 C
L ? - 4 Nov 1955 C
KOLOSAR, E 1879 - 22 Dec
1953 C
KOLOZYNSKI, Elerna 1868 -
29 Apr 1947 A
KOLUPA, Antoni 13 Jan 1851
- 20 Oct 1949 C
Wladyslawa 1860 - 27 Jan
1943 C (Nee: Majewski)
Stefan 1898 - 1913 C
KOLUPA, Michael -no
dates- F (Leokadya &
Mieczyslaw Janowski

KOLUPA (continued)
same lot)
KOMASINSKI, Michael 1886
- 12 Nov 1918 C
Mary J 1889 - 2 Apr 1967 C
(Nee: Piasecki)
KOMASINSKI, Frances 1838
- 12 Feb 1919 E
KONAPINSKI, Frank J 1875
husband - 20 Feb 1948 C
Frances 1884 wife - 4 June
1942 C (Nee: Jaworski)
Franciszek 1845 father -
1922 C
Katarzyna 1848 mother - 14
Apr 1924 C (Nee: Buc-
zynski)
Rose B 1880 - 1905 C
KONCZAN, Henrietta 1894 -
8 Dec 1967 A
Veronica 1855 - 1948 A
Jacob 1851 - 1920 A
Elizabeth 1885 - 1954 A
KONZEN, William E 1871 -
12 Mar 1947 A
KOPCZYNSKI, Antony Jr
1892 - 1918 WWI C
Mary 1874 mother - 1927 C
(Nee: Wrzeszcz)
Helen 1895 - 1900 C (Mar-
cin & Jozefa Wrzeszcz
same lot)
KOPINSKI, Catharine 1858 -
6 July 1946 C
KOPINSKI, Helen A 1892 - 4
Oct 1965 E
Michael C 1890 - 1 Dec
1969 E
KOPINSKI, Agnieszka ? mo-
ther - 1904 G
Michael 20 July 1866 father
- 7 Dec 1936 G
Clement ? - 1922 G
KORMOS, Theresa 1880 - 5
Aug 1939 C
KORNER, Anna 1871 - 16

KORNER (continued)
July 1943 C
Rudolph 1882 - 13 Dec 1952
C
KORNOWIECZ, Wladyslaw -
no dates- son C
Maryanna -no dates- daughter C
Ludwika 1856 - 1929 C
(Stanislaw Jagodzinski
same lot)
KORPAL, Roch J father -no
dates- D
Mary J 1867 mother - 27
Aug 1942 D (Nee: Krzeszewski)
Franciszek 8 Mar 1851 - 28
Mar 1888 D
Antony 1876 - 3 Apr 1939 D
Benjamin 1896 - 16 Sept
1968 D
M 1878 - 11 Nov 1954 D
J 1874 - 4 Aug 1955 D
KOSINSKI, Wanda sister -no
dates- C
Mary mother -no dates- C
Valentine Father -no dates-
C
Walter brother -no dates- C
KOSMATKA, Andrew 1813 -
1897 F
Michalena 1813 - 1909 F
Clara 1897 - 1964 F
KOSNOWSKI, Frank Dec
1870 - 5 June 1950 A
Leo 1900 - 13 Jan 1944 A
Apolonia 3 Feb 1871 - 20
July 1939 A (Nee: Rozplochowski)
KOSZEWSKI, Fred 1843
father - 1896 C
Jack 1876 son - 16 Aug
1940 C
Fred Jr 1880 son - 1930 C
Anna 1845 mother - 1910 C
(Nee: Podelwitz)

KOT, Mary 1882 mother -
1937 B
Paul J 1876 - 31 Aug 1952
B
KOTAL, Frank 1900 - 29
June 1960 E
KOTECKI, Max Aug 1895 -
1922 D
Frank D Oct 1891 - 15 July
1918 D "Killed in action -
Pvt Co A 8 Mach Gun"
Helen E 1874 - 1936 D
(Nee: Markiewicz)
Wladyslaw 1870 - 1931 D
(Joseph & Katharine Markiewicz same lot)
KOTZ, John 1877 - 21 Sept
1943 C
Theresa 1884 - 23 Nov 1964
C
KOTZENMACHER, Andrew
1883 - 17 Aug 1960 C
Barbara 1876 - 30 July 1951
C
KOVACH, Joseph 1922 - 1
Oct 1968 -
KOVACH, Catharine 1877 -
10 Sept 1969 -
KOVACH, Louis 1875 - 7
May 1943 A
KOVACH, Anton 1862 - 5
Apr 1939 C
KOVACH, Joseph P 1886 - 5
Dec 1952 D
KOVACH, Anna 1878 - 3 Dec
1947 G
KOVACH, Louis 1887 - 7
May 1949 E
KOVACH, Mary 1883 - 2
May 1963 C
KOVACS, Frank 1892 - 29
Aug 1945 B
KOVACS, Anna 1870 - 2 Apr
1947 G
J 1869 - 14 Nov 1954 G
"Died at Culver, IN"

35

KOVACSICS, Joseph 1892 -
12 Aug 1950 C
KOVACSICS, Alex 1884 - 20
July 1969 C
KOWALEK, Wladyslaw 1882
Son - 1885 D
Weronika 1887 daughter -
1904 D
Maryanna 1855 mother - 21
Oct 1938 D
Jan 1846 father - 1928 D
KOWALSKI, Magdeline 1815
mother - 1893 A
Joseph 1872 - 16 Sept 1939
A (Nicodem F, Apolonia,
& Anthony W Hosinski
same lot)
KOWALSKI, Frank 1874 -
1899 A
Matthew 1878 - 1902 A
Hattie 1889 - 1909 A
Nick 1848 father - 1927 A
Mary 1854 mother - 1930 A
Martha 1886 - 1949 A
KOWALSKI, Peter M ? - 15
May 1918 C "IN Pvt Coast
Arty Corps WWI"
Jozef 29 Oct 1848 - 14 Jan
1918 C
Anna 1868 - 11 May 1950 C
(Nee: Brekus) (Helen Ann
Mezykowski same lot)
KOWALSKI, Frank 20 Nov
1870 - 27 June 1871 D
KOWALSKI, Jozef 29 Nov
1860 - 15 Oct 1930 F
Maryanna 28 Dec 1863 - 5
Dec 1947 F
KOWALSKI, John 2 Aug 1887
- 25 July 1904 D
no name 27 Mar 1816
grandmother - 17 Nov 1900
D
Joseph L 1 Mar 1830 father
- 27 Mar 1893 D
Julia 1849 mother - 1921 D

KOWALSKI (continued)
(Nee: Wentland)
Joseph 16 Oct 1883 - 16
Nov 1884 D
Cecylia 12 Sept 1885 - 23
Oct 1886 D
David 31 Oct 1881 - 18 Mar
1899 D
Thomas 1881 - 1911 D
Clara 1898 - 22 Feb 1942 D
Richard 1 month old - 22
Feb 1942 D
KOWALSKI, Marcin 1852 -
1920 D
Katarzyna 1857 - 18 June
1944 D (Nee: Latosinski)
Frank Xavier 1873 - 23 Oct
1953 D
Frances 1890 - 1974 D
KOZAK, Theresa 1887 - mo-
ther - 30 Aug 1955 C
Joseph 1890 father - 15 Dec
1954 C
Anna 1916 daughter - 1936
C (Paul Horvath same lot)
KRAFT, John R 1916 - 23
Sept 1971 E
Mary 1878 - 30 Apr 1959 E
August Sr 1876 - 15 Mar
1953 E
KRAJEWSKI, Anna -no
dates- D
Stanislaw -no dates- D (Jan
& Katarzyna Witucki same
lot)
KRAKOWSKI, Irene 1919 -
1935 E
Bertha 1885 mother - 8 May
1968 E (Nee: Gluch)
Frank J 5 May 1913 - 5 Aug
1981 "Tec 5 US Army
WWII"
KRAKOWSKI, John L 1850 -
9 Dec 1908 A
Stanislaw 1874 son - 5 June
1925 A (six memorials on

36

KRAKOWSKI (continued)
this lot - not legible)
KRAMER, Nicholas J 1865 -
1935 B
Elizabeth 1861 - 1957 B
George N 1892 Son - 1925 B
KRAMER, Frank 1862 father
- 1922 B
Mary 1876 mother - 4 Apr
1945 B
Theresa 1885 - 26 July
1964 B
KRAMER, Elizabeth 1886 -
6 Sept 1973 B
Lawrence 1886 - 18 June
1949 B
Julia 1888 - 1931 B
M 1915 - 30 June 1955 B
(Mary Rose Kaman same
lot)
KRAMER, Mathias 1883 - 22
July 1957 G
Elizabeth 1884 - 24 Nov
1955 G
KRAMER, Caroline ? - 19
July 1910 H
KRANC, Frances 20 Jan 1896
mother - 12 Nov 1953 A
(Nee: Palicki)
KREGGER, Stella 1870 - 27
Sept 1940 C "Died at
Coldwater, MI"
KRISTOFSKI, Steven 1875
father - 1921 C
Margaret 1879 mother - 1
Feb 1939 C
KROEGER, Joseph 1883 - 22
Apr 1948 C
KROLL, Mamie 1888 - 19--
A (Margaret, Conrad, &
Maire Reider same lot)
KRONEWITTER, D 1945 -
21 July 1955 A
(Joseph, Katharine, Ber-
tha, Joseph, Stephen, &
Anna Wartha same lot)

KRUEGER, Josephine 1865 -
7 Nov 1944 A
KRUEPER, Paul Sr 1894 - 16
Nov 1968 -
KRUEZBERGER, Jacob J
1860 - 4 Dec 1938 A
KRUK, Johanna 24 Dec 1869
mother - 15 Apr 1924 C
(Nee: Wisniewski)
Joseph 1857 - 1924 C
Bronislawa 1890 - 1916 C
KRUK, Ladislaw 1870 father
- 1920 E
Mary 1866 mother - 1930 E
(Lawrence Sowala; Richard
Daniel Cook; & Stephen K
Gish same lot)
KRUPNIK, Joseph J 1914 -
1975 F "Pfc US Army
WWII"
Matilda 1912 - 19-- F
KRUSE, Stanley 1880 - 18
Oct 1939 C "Died at
Avilla, IN"
KRUSS, Frank 1879 - 3 Mar
1962 D
KRUSZYNSKI, Leo G 11 Apr
1896 - 25 Nov 1982 A
Amelia 29 Mar 1898 - 19
June 1932 A (Nee: Badur)
Mary 1896 mother - 1946 A
Joseph 1888 father - 1932 A
KRUZEL, Stanley 1871 - 15
Apr 1952 E
Mary 22 Mar 1872 - 3 Apr
1928 E (Nee: Dobrzykow-
ski)
KRZESZEWSKI (also SKR-
ZESZEWSKI), Wiktor F 1860
- 1912 D
Konstancya 2 Feb 1864 - 24
Sept 1864 - 24 Sept 1939 D
(Nee: Lukaszewski)
KRZESZEWSKI, Theresa
1898 - 23 Nov 1962 F
KRZYCHOWSKI, Estella Sz-

KRZYCHOWSKI (continued)
lanfucht 1907 - 13 Aug 1966 E "Mother & Grandmother" (Jan, Waleria, Jozefa, & Ludwig Szlanfucht same lot)
KUBIAK, Rev Ladislaw 1886 - 1912 Plaque on north side of Chapel "Ordained 1911 - son of Martin & Rose Kubiak"
KUBIAK, Hattie R 1895 - 1968 D
Stephen H 20 Aug 1887 - 18 Sept 1956 D "IN Cpl Co C 155 Inf"
Helen C 1894 - 15 Feb 1965 D
KUBIAK, Michael 1883 - 5 Feb 1958 D
Martha 1885 - 15 Feb 1965 (Nee: Mnichowski) D
KUBIAK, Jozefa -no dates- E
KUBIAK, Martin J -no dates- D
Jan -no dates- father D
Jozef -no dates- D
Pelegia -no dates- D
Antonina -no dates- mother D
Franciszek 1876 - 1913 D
Martin 1847 father 1911 D
Rose 11 Sept 1854 mother - 22 Apr 1936 D (Nee: Kominowski)
Bronislawa 1888 - 1917 D
KUBISIAK, Katarzyna 1857 mother - 23 June 1938 E (Nee: Klos)
Stanislawa 1895 - 1924 E
Stanislaw 1858 father - 1935 E
KUCHARICH, Theresa J 1890 - 31 Mar 1970 A
Martin 1887 - 7 Mar 1963 A

KUCHARSKI, Antoni 1852 - 1920 D
KUCHARSKI, Leon M 11 Nov 1864 - 20 Dec 1905 A
Edmund L 18 Nov 1889 - 31 Mar 1967 A "IN Cpl Btry C 344 Fld Arty"
Lottie 15 June 1866 mother 7 Dec 1949 A (Nee: Dobski)
Alfons 1899 - no date A
KUCHARSKI, Antonina 1844 - 1 Nov 1916 A (Nee: Wojciechowski)
Antony 1836 - 21 Dec 1900 A
KUCHARSKI, Stanislaw 4 May 1846 - 1923 D
KUJAWA, Jozef 1899 son - 1902 C
Maria 1893 daughter - 1960 C
Antoni 1861 father - 15 Apr 1930 C
Weronika 1872 mother - 9 May 1941 C
KUJAWA, Prakseda 1873 - 1920 D (Nee: Kubiak)
KUJAWA, Stanley 1885 - 29 Jan 1973 F
Wiktoria 27 Oct 1886 - 10 Oct 1917 F
KUJAWSKI, Ignatius 1836 father - 1908 C
J R 1893 - 1906 C
H R 1887 - 1908 C
Michalina 1836 mother - 1903 C
KUJAWSKI, Joseph 1895 - 22 Dec 1957 C
Veronika 1898 - 10 Sept 1954 C (Nee: Budnik)
KUJAWSKI, Martin 1864 father - 7 Feb 1953 C
Antonette 1862 mother - 20 Oct 1946 C (Nee: Las-

KUJAWSKI (continued)
kowski) "Married twice -
1st husband: Wojciech
Tajkowski, 2nd husband:
Martin Kujawski"
Leon 1907 - 1924 C
W 1890 - 1898 C
B 1889 - 1900 C (E & J
Tajkowski; & John Przy-
blinski, Jr same lot)
KUJAWSKI, Eleanore 13 Oct
1890 mother - 1922 A
(Nee: Kotolinski)
Del -no dates- A
Adam -no dates- A
Eve -no dates- A
Theodore -no dates- A
Tony 12 Dec 1877 father -
20 June 1966
KULCHER, Dennis 1874 - 17
Apr 1944 E
KUREK, Dorotea 1884 mother
- 1916 C
Mateusz 1877 father - 1954
C
KUREK, Jozef J 12 Mar 1873
- 9 Apr 1915 D (Anne
Kurek Hajducki same lot)
KUREK, John J 1879 father -
1931 D
Hedwige 1884 mother -
1929 D (Nee: Wisniew-
ski)
Casimir ? - 19 Feb 1935
"IN Fireman USNR"
KUREK, Jan 8 June 1848 - 9
Oct 1906 D
Maryanne 1 Feb 1847 - 6
Apr 1915 D
KUREK, Blanche 1879 - 14
Feb 1954 F (Nee: Cie-
sielski) (Stella, Florence,
& Lucya Ciesielski same
lot)
KURTIS, Martha 1874 - 2 Apr
1949 E

KUSNIEREK, Anna 1851 -
1898 D
Joseph 1880 - 1933 D
Jennie 1883 - 11 May 1965
D
KUZMIC, Matthew 1884 - 27
Jan 1969 -
KUZMIC, Elizabeth 1884 -
28 Sept 1961 D
KUZMICH, Paul 15 Jan 1839
- 6 Oct 1909 A
Apolonia 9 Feb 1858 - 31
Aug 1909
KUZMITZ, Katharine 1880 -
13 Oct 1964 A
KWIATKOWSKI, Martin 1873
father - 10 June 1948 C
Mary 1873 mother - 2 Dec
1943 C (Nee: Bladecki)
(Matthew Bladecki same
lot)
KWIATKOWSKI, Vincent -no
dates- C
Jan 1841 father - 1891 C
Anna 1850 mother - 1918 C
KWILAS, Jean F 1915
mother - 1972 C
Walter J 1912 - 1956 C
LADEWSKI, Martha 1891 -
11 May 1962 A
Wladyslaw 1885 - 13 June
1972 A
Loretta B 27 Oct 1917 - 8
Apr 1971 A "IN Y 2 US
Navy WWII"
LAGOCKI, Maryanna 1873
mother - 1925 A
Ignatius 1874 father - 3
July 1945 A (Katarzyna
Nowacki same lot)
LAKACKI, Petronella 1857 -
29 Dec 1949 C
LANKO, Frank 1886 - 24 Oct
1961 A
LARDNER, Jerome 1873 - 2
Feb 1947 Community

LARDNER (continued)
Cemetery ND
LASECKI, Steven 1899 - 18 June 1954 C
Amelia 23 Nov 1906 sister - no date C (Cecelia Broyles; & John & Frances Struck same lot)
LASECKI, Wojciech 1867 father - 1908 C
Anna 1874 mother - 1924 C (Nee: Strug)
Kazimiera 22 May 1892 - 19-- C
Helena 1 Aug 1895 - no date C
LASHBROUGH, Clara ? - 18 Jan 1952 B "Died in Logansport, IN"
LASKOWSKI, Rev Cornelius J 1910 - 30 Oct 1954 Interred in Chapel
LASKOWSKI, Pauline 1873 mother - 24 Apr 1952 A (Nee: Niezgodski)
Nicholas 1870 father - 13 July 1939 A
LASKOWSKI, Apolonia 1842 mother - 1922 A
Anna -no dates- A
Jozefa 1874 - 1955 A "Wife of Antony J Korpal"
Stanislawa 1878 - 1907 A
Katarzyna 1872 - 1910 A "Wife of John Hanyzewski"
John 1829 father - 20 July 1918 A
Stanley S 1908 - 9 May 1954 A
LASKOWSKI, Joseph N 1923 father - 1977 C "S1 US Navy WWII"
Loretta T 1924 mother - 19-- C
LASKOWSKI, Theodosia 3

LASKOWSKI (continued)
Jan 1868 - 6 Feb 1939 C (Nee: Dudek)
Henry Nov 1859 - 6 Oct 1904 C
LASKOWSKI, Michael Nov 1822 - 15 Apr 1904 D
Apolonia May 1835 - 21 May 1903 D
LASKOWSKI, K -no dates- E (Maryanna Andrzejewski same lot)
LASKOWSKI, Leonard 26 Nov 1920 - 21 Apr 1957 F "IN Tec4 857 Ord Heavy Maint Co WWII"
Antony -no dates- F
Ralph 1903 - 9 Oct 1955 F (Sylvester & Irene Marie Gonsiorowski same lot)
LASKOWSKI, Joseph John 29 Dec 1896 - 25 June 1961 F
Pauline G 1896 - 3 Apr 1959 F (Nee: Kubiak) (Casimir & Elaine Gary same lot)
LATOSINSKI, Antoni 11 May 1811 - 11 Nov 1888 D
Elizabeth 18 May 1821 - 22 Mar 1910 D (Antony Hazinski same lot)
LEBLANC, Peter 1885 - 27 Aug 1963 F
LECHNER, Margaret 1875 - 22 Aug 1951 C
Jacob 1873 - 18 May 1946 C
LEDA, Stella 1886 - 1920 C (Nee: Michor) (Wojciech & Maryanna Michor same lot)
LEDWICK, Michael 1946 - 5 Jan 1949 E
LEER, Frank 1885 - 23 Aug 1967 E
LEONARD, Josephine 1875 -

LEONARD (continued)
1904 A (Jacob & Helen Giersz same lot)
LEWALLEN, Joseph 1 day old - 18 Mar 1944 D
LEWANDOWSKI, Jozef 30 Sept 1867 - 6 July 1891 B
LEWANDOWSKI, Katarzyna 1853 - 1938 C
Wojciech 1850 - 1909 C
LEWANDOWSKI, Stephen W 31 Aug 1896 - 26 Sept 1918 C
Antony 1863 - 1904 C (Peter Szczypiorski same lot)
LEWANDOWSKI, Anna 1880 - 1927 C (Nee: Palicki)
Joseph 1879 - 24 Apr 1956 C
LEWANDOWSKI, Agnieszka 1852 - 1929 D (Nee: Machowiak)
LEWANDOWSKI, Franciszek 1842 - 1896 E
LEWINSKI, Leonard 1880 - 1907 F
Constantine 1865 father - 1914 F
Lottie 1867 mother - 30 June 1956 F (Nee: Kluszynski)
Hattie 1891 - 1927 F
LEWINSKI, Stanislaw K 1852 - 1934 D
Frances 1854 - 1908 D (Nee: Makowski)
Josephine 1880 - 11 Apr 1948 D
Sophia 1894 - 1935 D
LEWIS, Henry 1893 - 23 June 1939 D
LICHKAY, Andrew 1906 - 26 Sept 1960 H
LICHNOROWICZ, Christian 1917 - no date C

LICHNOROWICZ (continued)
Tillie 1868 mother - 1939 C (Nee: Wesolowski)
John 1918 - no date C
Edward L 29 Oct 1899 - 2 Jan 1952 C "IN S2 USNR WWI" (Irene & John Barber same lot)
LIGHT, Lillian 1895 - 21 July 1968 B
LIPECKI, Joseph 1861 - 26 Nov 1939 C
LISEK, Andrew ? father - 1895 F
Apolonia ? mother - 1907 F
LITZNIERSKI, Hattie 1888 - 28 July 1960 A
Leo S 1874 - 8 Nov 1939 A
LIWOSZ, Wiktorya 14 June 1876 - 11 May 1900 C (Mindykowski same lot)
LOCHMONDY, George 1889 - 26 Feb 1949 C
LOCHMONDY, Louis 1910 - 25 Sept 1958 A
LOCSMONDY, Elizabeth 1865 - 1 May 1941 C
LOLMAUGH, Anna 1869 - 28 Mar 1944 A
LONERGAN, John 1862 - 8 Nov 1955 D
Mary 1874 - 15 Nov 1945 D
LONZO, Anna 1873 - 13 Sept 1951 A "Died at Fort Wayne, IN"
LOOTENS, Albert 1868 - 28 July 1948 C
LORCH, Mike 1891 - 19 Oct 1957 D
LORDEN, John H 1891 - 12 Jan 1970 -
LOSHBOUGH, Lydia ? - 9 Aug 1943 A "Died at Wichita, KS"
LUCZKOWSKI, Joseph 1882 - 1907 C (Joseph Fezy &

41

LUCZKOWSKI (continued)
Lillian Nowakowski same
lot)
LUCZKOWSKI, Wladyslaw
June 1866 - 1920 C
Franciszka Mar 1866 - 6
Oct 1913 C (Nee: Graba-
rek)
Katharine 1905 - 1925 C
John 1906 - 14 Aug 1947 C
LUCZKOWSKI, Augusta July
1871 - 15 Dec 1964 E
(Nee: Walinski)
Stanislaw Aug 1875 - 21
May 1951 E
LUDWICZAK, Eddie 1882 -
13 Nov 1939 E
Rose 1891 - 1924 E (Nee:
Niewiadomy)
Frank 1887 - 1927 E (Piotr
& Maryanna Niewiadomy;
& Victory M Bogucki same
lot)
LUKASZEWSKI, John -no
dates- A
Eleanor 8 May 1897 - no
date A (Stanley, Frances,
& Blase Jaskowiak same
lot)
LUKASZEWSKI, Ignatius
1858 father - 1912 D
Antonette 1860 mother - 5
Oct 1938 D (Nee: Prawat)
LUKOWSKI, Clara 5 May
1897 - 22 Feb 1942 F
(Nee: Niespodziany) (Steve
& Josphine Niespodziany
same lot)
LUTHER, James 1871 - 21
May 1945 E
LUTHER, Cecelia 1869 - 18
Aug 1945 C
LUTHER, Mary 1875 - 3
Sept 1960 B
LUTTMAN, John 1878 - 4
Nov 1949 D

LUZNY, Jan 1857 - 1933 A
Franciszka 1857 - 1931 A
(Nee: Szymanski)
Kazimiera 1887 - 30 June
1970 A
LUZNY, Sophie K 1876 - 6
June 1958 A (Nee: Drejer)
Bruno 1866 - 1929 A
George 1902 husband - 31
Oct 1961 A (Jan & Fran-
ciszek Kolczynski same
lot)
LUZNY, Paul P 10 June 1888
- 20 May 1913 A
Pauline 1868 mother - 1933
A (Nee: Cach)
Roman 1859 father - 1937 A
Hattie 1897 - 6 Mar 1973 A
(Helen Luzny Guzicki
same lot)
LUZNY, Frank S 3 Sept 1852
- 9 Apr 1948 A
Antonina 1851 - 1926 A
(Nee: Kendziorski)
Angela G 1891 wife - 19--
A (Nee: Lukasiewicz)
Casimir F 1888 husband -
16 Oct 1947 A
LUZNY, Eugene Edwin 1921
- 10 July 1973 C
Antony 1876 - 27 May 1965
C
Salomea 1889 - 31 May
1949 C (Nee: Borkowski)
Edward L 1910 - 1921 C
LUZNY, Wanda 1894 - 27
Dec 1969 C
Clara B 1890 - 23 Aug 1961
C
Boleslaw 1857 - 7 Aug 1938
C
Antonina 1868 - 2 Dec 1928
C (Nee: Ginter) (Anna Gin-
ter same lot)
LUZNY, Alojzy 1917 - no
date F (Leokadya Grze-

LUZNY (continued) gorek same lot)
LUZNY, Helen H 1883 mother - 1955 F (Nee: Julek)
Casimir 1889 father - 19 Sept 1949 F
Joseph B 1919 - 1977 F
LYONS, Charles 1881 - 25 May 1942 -
LYNCH, Ellen 1870 - 19 Dec 1957 A "Died at Elkhart, IN"
LYNCH, Agnes 1876 - 8 Feb 1946 A "Died at Chicago, IL"
MACKOWIAK, Gail 2 days old - 18 Feb 1948 C
MADARAS, Agnes 1879 - 24 Dec 1958 D
A 1907 - 14 May 1954 D
MADARAS, Rose 1880 - 12 Apr 1962 A
MADDEN, Marian 1861 - 13 May 1940 D
MAGIERA, Esther 1912 - 20 Oct 1972 C
Josephine 1893 - 30 Mar 1968 C
Bert 1882 - 12 Apr 1972 C (no name Zgodzinski; Helen, Mary, & John Redling; S Dean Dombkiewicz; & Henrietta Woltman same lot)
MAHAR, Clara 1858 - 11 Feb 1944 D
Frank 1858 - 5 Jan 1939 D
MAHER, Anna 1837 - 1904 A
William Sr 1833 - 1896 A
MAHER, Rev F 1872 - 26 Jan 1947 Community Cemetery ND
MAIS, Bernard 1884 - 31 Aug 1963 G
Anna 1883 - 9 Feb 1963 G

MAJOR, Ethel 1880 - 28 Oct 1958 B
MAJOR, Alex 1878 - 2 Oct 1961 A "Died at Laredo, TX"
MAKIELSKI, no name 1861 - 1925 B (Tadeusz Janowiak; Michael & Josephine Rutowski; & John & Josephine Saberniak same lot)
MAKIELSKI, Mary H 1874 - 1912 C (Nee: Paczesny)
John P 1875 - 1934 C
William -no dates- C
Mamie -no dates- C
Modest -no dates- C
Anton 1879 - 1907 C
MAKIELSKI, Franciszek 1877 - 1909 D
Piotr 1854 father - 1901 D
Theophilia 1858 mother - 1934 D
Edward 1883 - 1887 D
Ludwig 1881 - 1882 D
Stephen J 1899 - 2 Nov 1964 D
Mamie 1896 - 1898 C
MAKIELSKI, Damazy -no dates- C (Peter & Helen Mroszkiewicz same lot)
MAKIELSKI, Edward F -no dates- E
Jacob F ? - 14 June 1904 E
Helen ? - 3 Oct 1947 E
John C 1907 - 13 June 1970 E
MAKOWSKI, Walenty ? father - 12 June 1888 D
Weronika daughter -no dates- D
MAKOWSKI, Alicya -no dates- G
Jan -no dates- G
Klemence -no dates- G
MAKOWSKI, Jozef 1885 son

MAKOWSKI (continued)
- 1917 H (Petronella Pie-
trzak & Teofilia Makow-
ski Wincek same lot)
MALAMY, W 1885 - 24 Jan
1957 -
MALCAINE, Mary T ? -
1971 -
MALECKI, Stephen 1875 -
1924 D
MALISZ, Frances C 1884 -
12 Aug 1925 A (Nee:
Gruszka)
Stephen J 1884 - 23 Sept
1941 A
Eva -no dates- A
Joseph -no dates- A
MALLON, Mary 1854 - 7
Mar 1940 A "Wife of
James Mallon"
MALONE, Grover ? - 11 Dec
1950 A
MANUSZAK, Waclaw 11
Sept 1893 husband - 1
June 1932 C
Katharine 7 Nov 1895 wife -
12 June 1973 C (Nee:
Szymkowiak)
Wojciech 23 Apr 1853
father - 17 Jan 1939 C
Mary 8 Dec 1859 mother -
19 June 1923 C
Kazimierz 26 Nov 1895 - 11
Dec 1921 C
Maryanna 9 Dec 1899 - 14
Apr 1900 C
Richard T 29 Mar 1925 -
19-- C
Michael 11 months old -
1940 C
MARCINIAK, Roman 1873 -
5 July 1949 A
Stella 1874 - 25 Feb 1961 A
Henry 1876 - 5 July 1956 A
Rozali 22 Aug 1850 mother
- 24 July 1901 A

MARCINIAK (continued)
Jan 1846 father - 1918 A
Leokadya -no dates- A
"Wife of Henry Marciniak,
Nee: Torzewski"
MARCINKOWSKI, Antoni
1893 father - 21 Jan 1970
E
Antonina 1896 mother -
19-- E (Joseph Stempin
same lot)
MARKIEWICZ, Katharine
1874 wife - 1 Feb 1939 C
"Wife of Frank Markie-
wicz"
MARKIEWICZ, Jozef 1838 -
1929 D
Katarzyna 1844 - 19-- D
(Helen, Wladyslaw, Max,
& Frank Kotecki same lot)
MARKOWSKI, Wladyslawa
1855 - 1 May 1942 C (Nee:
Pilarski)
Augustine -no dates- C
Sylvester 3 Dec 1885 - 17
Oct 1913 C
Jadwiga ? - 16 Jan 1916 C
Jozefa -no dates- C "Died
in Chiacgo, IL"
MARKOWSKI, August Jr
1894 - 8 June 1973 G
Edith 1898 - 18 Feb 1972 G
(Nee: Reed)
MARMS, Anna 1861 - 4 Nov
1947 A
MAROZSON, J 1884 - 7 Jan
1956 B
MARR, G ---- - 10 Sept
1955 Community Cemetery
ND
MARSHALL (See: Marszal),
Sophie M 1896 - 1975 C
Wladyslaw July 1872 father
- 1935 C
Bertha 1879 mother - 1919
(Nee: Niezgodski) C

44

MARSHALL, Matthew 14 Aug 1920 - 7 May 1981 E "US Navy WWII"
MARSHALL, Nellie 1880 mother - 11 Sept 1944 F
Alexander Joseph 1875 father - 24 Apr 1950 F
MARSZAL, no name -no dates- A
MARSZAL, Victor -no dates- D
Prakseda -no dates- D
Jozef -no dates- D
Blazy -no dates- D
Eloise 1887 - 2 Jan 1959 D
MARTHA, L 1871 - 9 Apr 1955 C
MARTINO, Joseph 1865 - 15 Jan 1947 E "Died at Berrien Springs, MI"
MARUSZEWSKI, Frances - - 1914 C
Wojciech 1854 - 1904 C
Stanislaw 1886 - 1904 C
(Marya Radaj same lot)
MARYASZ, Wojciech 23 Mar 1842 - 24 Aug 1889 D
Marya 25 Mar 1844 - 4 Apr 1918 D
MATERNOWSKI, John 1857 - 1895 F
MATHIS, Jacob 1858 - 23 Jan 1944 A
MATTASCHITZ, Mary 1886 - 12 Mar 1962 C
A ---- - 7 Feb 1955 C
MATTHEWS, A 1883 - 28 Oct 1953 A
MATTHEWS, Irene 1898 - 4 June 1945 A
Mary 1863 - 18 Dec 1940 A
MATUSZKIEWICZ, A 1878 - 9 Sept 1955 E
MAYO, no name baby - 10 Mar 1960 D
MAZURKIEWICZ, Matthew

MAZURKIEWICZ (cont.)
20 Aug 1891 - 9 Feb 1952 D "Ind Pfc Eng 7 Div WWI"
John 1868 - 25 Nov 1940 D
Katarzyna 1871 - 22 May 1940 D
MCALLISTER, Irene 1888 - 3 Jan 1970
John 1887 - 7 Jan 1972
MCBRIDE, Rev F 1883 - 8 June 1946 - Community Cemetery ND
MCBRIDE, Elizabeth 1867 - 16 July 1947 A
MCCAFFERTY, Rose 1864 - 27 Oct 1939 A "Died at Avilla, IN"
MCCARTHY, Thomas 1905 - 30 Sept 1962 E
MCCARTHY, Edward 1931 - 3 Sept 1973 -
MCCARTHY, Christine 1902 - 15 Jan 1969 - "Died at Kansas City, MO"
MCCARTHY, no name baby 28 Jan 1960 D
MCCARTHY, Mary Jane 1893 - 6 July 1952 A "Died at La Porte, IN"
MCCARTHNEY, Nellie A 1880 - 25 Dec 1971 - "Died at Michigan City, IN"
MCCARTHNY, J 1875 - 6 Oct 1945 A "Died at Dyer, IN"
MCCLANE, Christine 1872 - 25 Sept 1951 C "Died at Livonia, MI"
MCCREARY, Mary 1866 - 23 Oct 1943 A
MCDONALD, Mary 1850 - 29 May 1944 D
MCDONNELL, no name baby

45

MCDONNELL (continued)
1939 - 15 Dec 1941 E
MCEIHEDST, M 1868 - 22
Feb 1956 C "Died at Davi-
son, MI"
MCERLAIN, Frank E 1861 -
2 Sept 1948 B
Anna L 1864 - 21 Apr 1948
B
MCGARRITY, Timothy 10
days old - 1 Mar 1939 F
MCGINN, Rev John 1879 -
15 Sept 1948 Community
Cemetery NC
MCHALLECK (See: MI-
CHALEK), Stanley J ? 29
Feb 1932 A "IN Pvt 33 Inf
3 Div" (Chester Michalek
same lot)
MCHENRY, Jane 1863 - 12
Mar 1950 A
Owen 1868 - 5 May 1939 A
MCIVERNY, J I 1866 - 6
Dec 1954 D "Died at La
Porte, IN"
MCKEE, Minte ? 30 Sept
1968 -
MCKEE, Chester J 1896 - 18
Nov 1971 -
MCKEEL, Mary Martha 1864
- 28 Jan 1951 E
MCKEEN, Frederick T 1874
- 3 Sept 1950 Community
Cemetery ND
MCLAUGHLIN, K 1878 - 7
Nov 1955 D
MCMAHON, Lisa ? 2 Feb
1962 D
MCNAMARA, James 1944 -
1 Nov 1972 -
MCNAMARA, Caroline 1875
- 11 Aug 1957 A
Daniel J 1909 - 5 June 1967
A
Daniel 1878 - 15 Aug 1951
A

MCNAMARA (continued)
Kathryn 1880 - 8 Apr 1945
A
MCNAMARA, Mary 1914 -
14 Oct 1959 A
Sylvia 1899 - 23 Mar 1966
A
MCNAMARA, Margaret 1859
- 21 Jan 1946 A
Mary 1890 - 22 May 1941 A
MCNAMARA, John P 1864 -
7 Dec 1947 A
Catharine 1867 - 19 Jan
1944 A
no name 1859 - 13 Apr 1940
A
MCQUIRK, no name 1859 -
14 Mar 1939 D
MCTIGHE, Louise 1879 - 26
June 1959 G
MEDICH, Mildred 1885 - 31
Oct 1948 F
MEGAN, Bert 1876 - 9 June
1940 C
MEGYESI, Anna 1868 - 13
June 1947 D
MELTON, Elizabeth 1904 -
8 Sept 1959 G
MENDLIKOWSKI, no name -
no dates- E
MENDLIKOWSKI, Kswary
father -no dates- F
Wiktorya mother -no dates-
F (Nee: Witucki)
Kazimiera -no dates- F
Prakseda 1880 - 29 Jan
1958 F
Czeslaw 1877 - 6 Aug 1947
F
MENYHART, M 1874 - 22
Nov 1954 C
Charles ? - 20 Apr 1948 C
MESAROS, Stephen 1889 - 4
Oct 1961 D
METCALF, baby stillborn -
24 May 1971 - "Died at

METCALF (continued)
Dearborn, MI"
MEUNINCK, Charles 1859 -
11 Sept 1947 C
MEZYKOWSKI, Helen Ann
1907 - 1935 C (Peter &
Jozef Kowalski same lot)
MEZZEI, E 1917 - 3 Dec
1954 -
MEZZI, John 1883 - 2 Sept
1947 D
MICHALEK, Chester 1912 -
1921 A (Stanley McHal-
leck same lot)
MICHALY, (Mike) Peter
1866 - 7 Nov 1946 C
MICHALSKI, Josef 1869
father - 1927 C
Josephine 1871 mother - 4
Aug 1960 (Nee: Habitzki)
C
Leon 1896 - 1918 C
Jan ? father - 18 Feb 1900
C
Wladyslaw 5 Oct 1907 - 9
Nov 1938 C
MICHALSKI, John 24 June
1813 - 21 Oct 1911 -
MICHALSKI, Martin 1873 -
1924 E
Anna J 1876 - 1925 E
MICHOR, Maryanna 1859 -
28 Apr 1944 C
Wojciech 1853 - 1916 C
(Stella Michor Leda same
lot)
MICINSKI, Vincent 1845 - 24
Dec 1917 A
Jozefa 3 Mar 1872 - 1898 A
Ignacy 27 July 1871 - 1928
A (Wojciech Witkowski
same lot)
MICINSKI, Ladislaw 1864 -
22 May 1941 C
Agnes 1866 - 22 July 1956
C

MICINSKI (continued)
Stanley 1894 - 14 Sept 1948
C
Clement 1907 - 4 Feb 1972
C
MICINSKI, Constance 1878 -
27 Feb 1949 E (Nee: Fry-
drych)
John L 1874 - 1963 E
MIKESELL, Margaret 1873 -
21 Sept 1958 H
MIKLASZEWSKI, Rev M
1850 - 21 May 1917 B
"Plaque on South Side of
Chapel"
MIKO, Anna 1892 - 15 Apr
1964 G
Stephen 1885 - 31 Mar 1967
G
MIKO, Anna 1869 - 22 Dec
1943 F
Katharine 1906 - 16 Oct
1940 F
MIKOLAJCZAK, Maryanna
-no dates- D
MILLER, Lewis V 1882 hus-
band - 1954 D
Bertha 1882 wife - 1936 D
(Nee: Palicki) (Stanley &
Helen Palicki; Szyman &
Konstancya Palicki; Jo-
seph & Anna Wroblewski;
& Joseph & Regia Stacho-
wiak same lot)
MILLER, Frank 18 Apr 1856
- 15 July 1918 F
MILLER, M 1861 - 25 Jan
1955 C
Otto Sr 1887 - 23 Feb 1946
C
MILLER, Thomas L 1868 -
24 Oct 1942 A
F 1908 - 28 Nov 1955 A
MILLER, Joseph 1884 - 29
Aug 1941 D
Michael ? - 21 July 1962 D

MILLER, Ada 1874 - 23 Dec
1961 B
MILNAR, Anna 1880 - 24
Dec 1959 B
MILTENBERGER, Helen
1937 - 2 Feb 1945 -
MILTENBERGER, Theresa
1906 - 17 Mar 1971 -
"Died at Goshen, IN"
MILTENBERGER, infant
26 July 1938 D
MILTENBERGER, Daniel J
1919 - 24 Aug 1942 -
MINDYKOWSKI, no name -
no dates- C (Wiktorya
Liwosz same lot)
MISCHKER, Maryann 1876 -
4 Aug 1939 A
Victoria 1893 - 30 Aug 1964
A
MITTERMAYER, B 1903 - 2
Nov 1949 Community
Cemetery ND
MITTERMAYER, Ignaz 1879
- 13 July 1951 C
MNICHOWSKI, Stanislawa J
1874 mother - 7 Jan 1969
B
Stanislaw 1869 father - 10
Nov 1940 B (Alex, Frances
F, Maryanna, & Roman J
Sledzikowski same lot)
MNICHOWSKI, Boleslaw
186- - (dates illegible) D
Katarzyna -no dates- D
(Nee: Kubiszewski)
MNICHOWSKI, George 1818
- 1903 D
Agnes 1822 - 1904 D
MNICHOWSKI, S W 1866 -
1925 D
Stephen 1863 - 1913 D
Helena 1908 - 1908 D
Wladyslaw 1890 - 1891 D
MODORY, Elizabeth 1881 -
31 Dec 1961 B

MODORY (continued)
C J 1872 - 28 Oct 1955 B
MOFFETT, Catharine 1862 -
30 Jan 1939 C
MOLLOY, Mary A 1851 - 23
Dec 1942 - "Wife of Frank
Molloy"
MOLNAR, Rose 1867 - 13
Aug 1938 A
MOLNAR, Sidonia 1880 - 24
July 1945 B
Louis 1879 - 12 Nov 1961 B
MOLNAR, Louis 1890 - 7
Apr 1959 D
Ethel 1898 - 2 July 1970 D
MOONEY, Teresa 1881 - 26
Sept 1950 D "Died at St
Louis, MO"
MOORE, Mary ? - 17 June
1957 C "Died at Chicago,
IL"
MORAN, Ida 1871 - 10 May
1964 A
MORENCE, Thomas A baby
- 4 Jan 1949 E
MORSE, Franklin 1897 - 15
Mar 1972 G
Claire 1900 - 17 Oct 1960 G
MOYIHAN, Jerry 1864 - 17
Aug 1943 -
MOZYNSKI, Stanislawa 19
July 1874 - 27 Aug 1900 F
(Nee: Wroblewski)
Franciszek 30 Mar 1873 -
1893 F (Wladyslaw Dob-
rzykowski same lot)
MROCZEK, S 1890 - 29 Nov
1953 C
MRUCZKIEWICZ, Peter
1875 - 1946 C
Helen 1870 - 1950 C (Dam-
azy Makielski same lot)
MROZAK, Anna ? - 1917 E
MROZINSKI, Walter E 1896
father - 22 Feb 1940 D "IN
Pfc 309 Eng 84 Div PH"

48

MROZINSKI (continued)
Sophie 1894 mother - 1980
D (Nee: Rowinski)
MUCKENTHALER, Leo J
1893 - 12 Feb 1950 A
"Died at Lucas Co, OH"
MUELLER, Elizabeth 1885 -
15 June 1949 B
MUELLER, Mae 1900 - 19
May 1971 F
J 1894 - 2 Jan 1957 F
MUELLNER, Joseph 1868 -
18 Feb 1951 F
E 1868 - 30 Sept 1954 F
MUGHL, Teresa 1887 - 24
May 1962 C
MUHL, John 1872 - 6 Nov
1954 Community Cemetery
ND
MUINCH, Mary J 1873 - 19
June 1964 D
MULLIGAN, Paul 1897 - 12
Apr 1959 A
Joseph 1887 - 1 June 1941
A
MULLINS, Lawrence A 1909
- 10 Aug 1969 A
MULLINS, Patrick 1 day old
- 5 July 1941 A
MURPHY, Ann 1886 - 20
Oct 1961 D
MURPHY, Loretta 1886 - 17
May 1961 D
MUSZIK or MUSZIAK, no
name baby ---- - 10 Mar
1943 F
Julius 1884 father - 9 Sept
1940 F
Frances 1890 mother - 18
Mar 1942 F
MYERS, Sadie 1877 - 24
July 1944 A
MYSKA, Michael 1817 -
1906 C (Antoni & Mary-
anna Smoger same lot)
NAFRADY, John 1906 - 28

NAFRADY (continued)
Jan 1946 C
NAGY, Mary 1893 - 21 Oct
1946 E
NAGY, Joseph 1890 - 25 Oct
1963 E
Mary 1891 - 19 June 1971 E
NAGY, J 1883 - 3 Mar 1954
E
J 1886 - 4 Apr 1957 E (John
Hanyzewski same lot)
NAPIERALSKI, Stephen 1891
- 1928 G
Anna 1893 - 19-- G (Nee:
Gierzynski)
NATKIEWICZ, Albin C 1894
- 18 Jan 1955 F
Bernice H 1893 - 21 Feb
1972 F
NATKIEWICZ, John 1863 -
20 Aug 1943 B
John M 1899 son - 1943 B
Teresa 1868 mother - 22
Feb 1950 B
Casimir 1861 father - 1937
B
NEDDO, J N 1877 - 25 Oct
1954 B
NEENAN, Adeline 1884 - 26
July 1950 B
NEMETH, Elizabeth 1882 -
8 Nov 1942 A
NEMETH, Steve P 1884 - 13
Apr 1951 C
NEMETH, F 1877 - 12 Dec
1956 C
NEMETH, Verna 1886 - 7
Aug 1961 C
NEMETH, Charles 1887 - 29
Dec 1971 -
NEMETH, G 1894 - 3 May
1953 D
Mary 1895 - 6 May 1949 D
NEMETH, Rose 1874 - 28
Apr 1956 D
NEMETH, Steven 1881 - 29

NEMETH (continued)
Feb 1944 D
Steve 1866 - 28 Feb 1945 D
NEMETH, Katharine Papai
1872 - 16 Mar 1952 D
NEMETH, Rozalia 1886 - 26
Apr 1949 E
Frank 1880 - 21 Nov 1964 E
NEMETH, George G 1912 -
12 Apr 1966 F
NEMETH, Mary 1886 - 15
Apr 1962 G
NEWMAN, E 1867 - 17 Nov
1954 A
NIEDBALSKI, Catharine 1863
mother - 1925 A (Nee:
Szybowicz)
Vincent 1858 father - 23
Apr 1908 A
Pauline 1893 - 18 Aug 1941
A
Julius V 1894 - 9 Jan 1939
A
NIEDBALSKI, Karol 1848 -
1912 A
Suzanna 1852 - 19-- A
(Nee: Sieradzki)
Agnes 8 Jan 1888 - 1 July
1970 A (Nee: Kendzior-
ski)
John 27 Oct 1875 - 1932 A
Jadwiga 1889 - 28 Dec 1908
A (Emery & Emery A Jr
Fredericks same lot)
NIEDBALSKI, Wladyslaw
1901 - 1922 C
Marcin 11 Nov 1848 - 7 Apr
1936 C
Marya 8 July 1868 - 30 Aug
1952 C (Nee: Szybowicz)
NIEDBALSKI, Hattie 1886 -
30 Oct 1943 D (Nee: Kala-
majski)
Leo J 1883 - 5 Jan 1946 D
NIEDBALSKI, no name -no
dates- E

NIEDBALSKI, no name -no
dates- F
NIEDBALSKI, Leonard M 13
Jan 1925 - 3 May 1945 G
"Marine Pfc, killed in ac-
tion on Iwo Jima"
Clementine Niedbalski
Radziszewski "Gold Star
Mother" 1902 - 1964 G
Sylvester 1897 - 5 Dec 1942
G
NIEDZIELSKI, Ignacy 1870 -
22 Nov 1957 F
Marta 1880 - 15 July 1963
F (Nee: Deka) (John &
Anna Deka same lot)
NIEMIER, Kazimiera Pie-
chocka "Wife of Peter F
Niemier" 1893 - 1918 F
(Michael & Wladyslawa
Piechocki same lot)
NIESPODZIANY, Rozalia
1864 - 1917 C
Frank 1887 - 24 July 1961
C
Nicholas 1870 - 17 Dec
1963 C
NIESPODZIANY, Walenty
1869 - 22 Nov 1938 E
Alojzy 1897 - 1903 E
Katarzyna 1868 - 1934 E
(Nee: Komasinski)
Bronislaw 1895 - 1904 E
Martha 1903 mother - 12
Nov 1942 E
no name mother -no dates-
E
Nicholas 1862 father - 29
Mar 1942 E
Clement 1901 father - 22
July 1940 E
NIESPODZIANY, Josephine
1870 mother - 1930 F
(Nee: Czajkowski)
Stephen 1870 father 1909 F
(Clara Lukowski same lot)

NIESPODZIANY, Anna 1870
- 1927 F
NIEWIADOMY, Piotr 1856 -
1920 E
Maryanna 1860 wife - 1921
E (Frank & Rose Lud-
wiczak; & Victoria Bo-
gucki same lot)
NIEZGODSKI, Stanley 1910 -
1954 H
Sadie 1875 - 14 Dec 1956 H
NIEZGODSKI, Stanley 27 Oct
1883 - 1956 A
Jan 20 Mar 1853 - 1926 A
Maryanna 19 June 1854 - 13
Oct 1900 A
Vincent 1882 - 1927 A
(Frances Zakaszewski
same lot)
NIEZGODSKI, Mary 1874 -
27 Nov 1944 A
Ignacy 1871 - 16 Feb 1917
A
Joanna 1870 - 29 Jan 1907
A
Jozef 1841 - 27 Apr 1904 A
NIEZGODSKI, Casimir 1846
- 10 Aug 1904 C
Magdeline 1856 - 1927 C
NIEZGODSKI, Henry A 1903
husband - 1937 D
Jozef 1872 brother - 8 Apr
1918 D
Stephania 1905 - 1912 D
Agnes 1828 mother - 1910
D
Adam 1902 - 1902 D
Alojzy 1900 - 1904 D
Tekla 1875 wife - 2 Dec
1965 D (Nee: Buczkow-
ski)
John T 1872 husband - 18
June 1961 D
NIEZGODSKI, Valaria 1878 -
12 Aug 1946 D
Katarzyna 5 Nov 1841 - 18

NIEZGODSKI (continued)
Nov 1924 D (Nee: Palicki)
Kazimierz 1844 - 1921 D
Wanda 1883 - 3 Aug 1944 D
(Nee: Kalajmajski)
NIEZGODSKI, Jacenty 1834
father - 1919 D
Maryanna 1839 mother -
1933 D
Teofil 1877 - 30 Sept 1913
D
Wladyslawa -no dates- D
Ludwik -no dates- D
Zygmond 7 Apr 1877 - 21
July 1941 D
NIEZGODSKI, Constance
1866 mother - 29 Oct 1918
E (Nee: Woltman)
NIEZGODSKI, Frank 1849 -
1896 F
Jozefa 1865 - 1913 F (Nee:
Palicki)
Martha M 1893 - 20 Aug
1956 F
Juliana 1896 - 29 June 1911
F
NITKA, Michael 1857 - 13
Sept 1902 C
Constance 1861 - 21 Dec
1945 C (Stephen, Salomea,
Andrzej, & Agnieszka Spy-
chalski same lot)
NIVEN, Ellen 1872 - 25 Nov
1949 C
Albert 1903 - 18 June 1966
C
Wm Calvin 1861 - 3 Apr
1951 C
NIVEN, Anna 1865 - 27 June
1938 A "Wife of Edward
Niven"
NIXON, Roy A 1902 - 12 Oct
1972 - "Died at Marco Is-
land, FL"
NOBLE, Angelo 1870 - 11
Nov 1940 A

NOBLE (continued)
Catharine 1872 - 31 July 1941 A
NORRIS, R 1899 - 15 Dec 1955 Community Cemetery ND
NORTH, William and Michael (twins) 18 Sept 1961 A (Jacob, Helen, Leo, & Josephine Janowiak; Joseph Wcisel; Helen Hosinski; & Michael Baloun same lot)
NORTON, Mary 1877 - 14 Dec 1946 C
NOWACKI, Michael 1843 father - 1895 F (Rozalia & Wincenty Wozniak same lot)
NOWACKI, Katarzyna ? - 3 July 1913 F (Maryanna Lagocki same lot)
NOWACKI, Maryanna 1867 mother - 1946 C
Piotr 1867 father - 1936 C
Martha 1901 - 1903 C
NOWACZEWSKI, infant 8 Aug 1948 - 8 Aug 1948 F
T ? - 30 May 1950 F
NOWACZEWSKI, Clementine 24 May 1940 - 25 May 1940 D
NOWAK, Eligius 1900 - 1920 A
Julia 1876 - 22 May 1942 A
Stanley 1875 - 30 July 1940 A
NOWAK, Mary 1867 - 15 Nov 1946 C
NOWAK, Stanley J 1884 - 11 Oct 1941 D
Pelegia 1886 - 33 Jan 1957 D (Nee: Gonsiorowski)
NOWAK, Paulina 1851 - 1919 D
Josef 1851 - 1921 D

NOWAK, Antonette ? - 26 Sept 1948 E
Joseph P 1870 - 1933 E
NOWAK, Theresa 1887 mother - 2 Jan 1962 G
John 8 May 1884 - 15 June 1962 G "MI CWT US Navy WWI & WWII"
NOWAKOWSKI, Alex 1879 - 26 July 1940 A "Died at Racine, WI"
Wladyslawa 1884 - 14 Aug 1970 A (Nee: Woodka)
NOWAKOWSKI, Leokadya 1884 - 27 Aug 1973 C (Nee: Luczkowski)
Stanislawa baby -no dates- C
Joseph 1888 - 22 July 1948 C (Joseph Luczkowski & Joseph J Fezy same lot)
NOWAKOWSKI, Jan July 1854 father - no date G
Rozalia Aug 1854 mother - 27 Mar 1909 G (Nee: Skolecki)
Bill son -no dates- G
Steve 1940 - 10 Oct 1958 G
NOWINSKI, Nikodem 1844 grandfather - 1920 E
Maryanna 1840 sister - 1923 E
Julianna 1845 grandmother - 1923 E
Nick 1866 - 1933 E (Wladyslaw Wesolowski same lot)
NURKOWSKI, Joseph 1888 - 1948 E
Mary 1892 - 17 May 1965 E
Richard 1932 - 31 Oct 1959 E
Joseph M 1914 - 17 Nov 1940 E
NYERGES, John 1893 - 8 Nov 1964 A

NYERGES (continued)
Agnes 1890 - 8 May 1969 A
NYERGES, A 1888 - 30 Oct
1954 B
NYIKOS, Anna G 1905 - 14
Mar 1971 -
NYIKOS, Rose M 1895 - 8
July 1967 C
NYIKOS, J 1893 - 16 June
1954 E
NYIKOS, Barbara 1873 - 22
Jan 1951 G
OBARSKI, Julia 1900 - 17
Jan 1967 E
Frank B 22 Nov 1897 - 9
May 1963 E "IN Pvt US
Army WWI"
Helen 1895 - 29 Dec 1899 E
(Anna Pilarski; & Clement
& Alexander Paege same
lot)
OBER, Antony 1843 - 1928 C
Tillie 1847 - 1926 C
Edward C 1898 - 6 Apr 1938
C
Victor ? - 10 Nov 1906 C
Mary ? - 10 Nov 1906 C
(Ferdinand & Sophie Gra-
bowski same lot)
OBRIEN, John 1863 - 7 July
1957 A
Francis 1884 - 3 Feb 1950
A "Died at La Porte, IN"
OBRIEN, Margaret G 1888 -
15 Sept 1966 A "Died at
Chicago, IL"
Frank 1882 - 10 Apr 1939 A
"Died at Chicago, IL"
George F Sr 1867 - 11 Nov
1942 A
Helen 1880 - 25 Feb 1943 A
George L 1873 - 20 Dec
1943 A
Pat 1925 - 21 Jan 1948 A
"Died at Chicago, IL"
Katharine 1874 - 1 Apr 1948

OBRIEN (continued)
A
OBRIEN, George 1893 - 15
Oct 1959 E
OBRIEN, B Angela 1860 - 2
June 1938 C
OBRIEN, F T 1900 - 29 Nov
1944 F
ODONNEL, Rebecca ? - 29
Mar 1960 F
baby age 1 12 Mar 1961 F
ODONNEL, Katharyn 1870 -
21 Jan 1950 A
Michael J 1868 - 24 Dec
1938 A
ODONNELL, Thecla age 3
months 30 May 1964 -
ODONNELL, Anna 1885 - 12
Jan 1968 D
Edward 1884 - 16 Feb 1968
D
infant 20 Oct 1946 D
ODONNELL, Rev Hugh 1895
- 16 June 1947 Community
Cemetery ND
ODOR, Helen 1872 - 25 Mar
1956 G
Elek 1870 - 24 Apr 1945 G
OGNISZAK, Napomucena
1858 - 1906 C (Nee: Buc-
zkowski)
Martin 1855 - 1914 C (Ade-
line S Policinski same lot)
OGURKIEWICZ, Anthony J
1858 - 1912 E
Sylvestor 17 Oct 1885 - no
date E "Son of A J & W A
Ogurkiewicz"
OLAWSKI, Leo J 1912 - 15
Feb 1952 C "Pfc US Army
WWII"
Valentine 1878 father - 30
Aug 1946 C
Josephine 1878 mother - 5
Aug 1951 C (Nee: Kwiat-
kowski)

OLEJNICZAK, Magdelena 1897 - 1902 E
Edward 1904 husband, son – 1934 E
Mary 1864 mother - 12 Nov 1941 E (Nee: Gierzynski)
Joseph 1854 father - 1931 E
Piotr 1820 grandfather - 1904 E
OLSON, Edith 1878 - 9 Apr 1967 D
ONEIL, Roland 1895 - 27 Aug 1960 B
ONEIL, Sarah 1872 - 14 Nov 1943 D
ONEIL, Mary 1864 - 8 Mar 1950 D
ORBAN, no name 1873 - 1937 C
Victoria 1883 - 18 Sept 1946 C
Charles 1902 - 29 July 1946 C (Victoria, Charles J, Paul, Elizabeth, & Charles Kalman same lot)
OREILLY, Edwin 1870 - 19 Feb 1945 G
Lucy 1878 - 11 May 1951 G
ORNAT, Mary 10 Aug 1874 - 8 Sept 1939 D (Antony, Leon, Joseph B Wyremblewski; & Jacob Wozniak same lot)
OSBORN, Robert E 1909 - 25 July 1973 -
OSHEA, Rev Dennis 1888 - 3 July 1948 Community Cemetery ND
OSHEA, John 1884 - 19 Nov 1949 D
William J 1888 - 27 Sept 1951 D "Died at Oak Forest, IL"
OSWALD, Michael F 1876 - 5 June 1949 Community Cemetery ND

OTOLSKI, Mary 23 Sept 1892 - 6 Apr 1923 - (Nee: Filipiak) "Wife of Joseph F Otolski"
F 1859 father - 1902 -
OTOLSKI, Michael L 1891 - 1911 C
Eleanora 1855 mother - 1916 C (Telesfore & Amelia Radomski; & Joseph & Blondine Smiecinski same lot)
OTOOLE, Margaret 1871 - 15 Dec 1959 D "Died at Alpena, MI"
OWEN, Elizabeth D 1885 - 18 Jan 1973 D
Thomas F 1882 - 25 Jan 1949 D
PAAR, Alex 1886 - 9 May 1963 A
Pauline 1885 - 29 Aug 1965 A
PACZESNY, Michael 1866 - 18 Feb 1946 C
Mary 1873 - 1936 C
Heromin -no dates- C
Weronika -no dates- C
Genowefa -no dates- C
PACZESNY, Katharine 1875 - 30 May 1945 D
Andrew F 1872 - 18 Apr 1951 D
PAEGE, Clement 1912 - 1916 E
Alexander Jr baby - 1909 E (Julia, Frank B, Helena Obarski; & Anna Pilarski same lot)
PALFI, Katharine 1862 - 10 Nov 1951 C
PALI, Mary 1875 - 18 Mar 1939 C
PALICKI, Stanislawa 3 June 1876 - 7 Oct 1904 C
Wilhelmina 1833 - 1921 C

PALICKI (continued)
(Prakseda & Jan Pulaski
same lot)
PALICKI, Waclaw 28 Nov
1876 brother - 19 Jan 1904
C
Piotr 14 Feb 1874 - 24 Aug
1910 C
Marya 16 Aug 1837 mother
- 30 July 1905 C
Adalbert 1840 father - 1922
C
PALICKI, Raymond 1905 -
19-- D
Helen 1907 - 19-- D
PALICKI, Helen 1899 mother
- 21 Apr 1942 D
Stanley 1890 father - 17
June 1970 D (Lewis V Mil-
ler same lot)
PALICKI, Szymon 1851 -
1924 D
Konstancya 1855 - 1922 D
(Joseph & Anna Wroblew-
ski; Bertha Miller; & Jo-
seph & Regina Stachowiak
same lot)
PALICKI, Stanley 1897 -
1921 D
Mary 1893 - 1899 D
PALICKI, Martin 1848 - 1901
F
Julia 1843 - 1929 F (Nee:
Wawrzyniak)
Paul 1882 - 1936 F
PALKA, Walter M Feb 1884
- 25 Mar 1951 A
Hattie 1885 - 25 Nov 1972
A (Nee: Niezgodski)
Irene 1904 daughter - 1917
A
PALLITIN, Katharine 1891 -
17 June 1970 -
PALLO, Mary 1887 - 16 Oct
1972 -
PALLO, Shirley 7 months old

PALLO (continued)
- 12 Jan 1949 C
PAPAI, Frank 1884 - 20 Nov
1943 B
Elizabeth 1889 - 12 Dec
1941 B
PAPAI, B 1883 - 11 June
1954 -
PAPAY, Rose 1891 - 4 Mar
1961 C
Stephen 1870 - 3 Jan 1942
C
PAPAY, Stephen F 1879 - 2
Jan 1951 A
PAPCZYNSKI, Bronislawa
1874 - 1900 B (Nee: Ko-
walski)
Teresa 1898 - 1899 B
John W 1869 - 1911 B
PARADIC, Verona Toth 1891
- 27 June 1971 E
Joseph 1885 - 7 Mar 1963 E
PARRISH, Clarence 1898 - 6
Sept 1971 H
Anna R 1904 - 3 May 1969
H
PASZEK, George F 24 Mar
1876 - 25 Dec 1936 D
Lottie S 1886 - 26 Aug 1952
D (Nee: Przybysz)
PASZEK, Joseph ? father -
no date D
Mary ? mother - no date D
(Nee: Pilarski) (Mary M
Beyer same lot)
PASZKIET, Josephine 13
Mar 1896 - 8 July 1939 D
"Wife of Leo Paszkiet,
nee: Szotynski"
PAUL, Leon ? - 21 Sept 1938
A
PAULIN, Harry 1882 - 24
June 1957 B
Mae R 1883 - 12 Mar 1966
B
PAWLAK, Justyna 2 Dec

PAWLAK (continued)
1821 – (date illegible) D
PAWLICKI, John 1880 – 1972 A
Mary 1881 – 7 Jan 1970 A
PAWLICKI, Louis 1904 – 1974 B
Mary 1881 – 7 Jan 1970 B
PAWLICKI, Marcin 1848 father – 1901 E
Franciszek 1848 mother – 1925 E
PECSI, John 1880 – 22 Apr 1947 C
PENDEL, Joseph A 1901 – 7 May 1949 A
Emmanuel 1866 – 25 Feb 1941 A
Julia 1867 – 1 Dec 1939 A
PERLEY, Harold O 1902 – 19 May 1970 –
PERLEY, Arthur 1863 – 14 Dec 1961 A
Agnes 1874 – 9 Aug 1966 A
PETERSON, Charles 1859 – 1918 A
Julia 1865 – 8 Aug 1949 A (Mary J Arndt (daughter) same lot)
PHELAN, Frances J 1867 – 1 June 1947 Community Cemetery ND
PHILION, Miranda 1849 – 12 Sept 1940 E
PHILION, William 1873 – 18 Mar 1942 B
PIANOWSKI, Stephen 1867 father – 1929 G
Mary 1872 mother – 25 Mar 1946 G
Leo J 1910 – 2 Feb 1972 G
Lillian V 1908 – 19-- G
PIASECKI, Sally 1877 – 4 Jan 1957 C (Nee: Woltman)
Stanislaus 1863 – 10 Nov

PIASECKI (continued)
1951 C
PIASECKI, Jozef 1852 father – 1898 D
Salomea 1854 mother – 1918 D (Nee: Zakrzewski)
Bronislaw 1884 – 1888 D
Wladyslawa Helena –no dates– D
Jadwiga 1882 – 1900 D
Frank 1880 – 11 Jan 1952 D
PIASECKI, Wladyslawa 1887 – 31 May 1964 D (Nee: Wroblewski)
Leo 1883 – 22 Mar 1961 D
PIASECKI, John 1886 – 29 Nov 1962 F
Mary 1887 – 5 June 1961 F (Nee: Kruk)
Heromin 1909 – 1917 F
Jean Mae infant 10 days old – 27 Dec 1938 F
PIASECKI, Joseph 1848 father – 1897 F
Agnes 1856 mother – 1934 F
Antony 1893 – 1910 F (Anna Plocki same lot)
PIASECKI, Irene 1891 – 1934 F (Nee: Bykowski)
Teofil 1856 father – 7 Dec 1932 F
Pelegia M 30 May 1864 – 6 May 1897 F (Nee: Kobecki)
Lucya –no dates– F
PIECHOCKI, Alozy 1908 son – 1920 F
Michael 1871 father – 26 Dec 1942 F
Wladyslawa 1872 mother – 1936 F
Kazimiera Niemier 1892 – 1918 F "Wife of Peter Niemier"
Joseph infant 1 day old – 25

PIECHOCKI (continued)
Aug 1940 F
PIECHOROWSKI, Frank
1890 father - 1928 H
Leokadya 1883 mother -
1935 H (Nee: Hosinski)
PIECHOROWSKI, Stanislawa
1880 - 1935 H (Nee: Ho-
sinski)
Wladyslaw 1874 father - 8
Feb 1941 H
Helen Marie 1911 - 11 Dec
1949 H
PIECHOROWSKI, Virgil B 2
Aug 1931 - 16 Jan 1975 C
"US Army Korean War"
Peter Jr 19 Feb 1925 - 24
Feb 1945 C "Marine, kill-
ed in action on Iwo Jima"
Peter J Sr 23 Mar 1887 - 26
May 1974 C
Helen 10 Apr 1890 - 17 Dec
1977 C (Nee: Leszcz)
"Married 24 Sept 1912"
PIENIAZKIEWICZ, Jozefa
1849 mother - 1937 C
Joseph D 1860 son - 4 May
1908 C (Mary, Sylvester,
Helen, & Elge D Gon-
siorowski same lot)
PIERCE, Ola W 1881 - 21
July 1950 C "Died at
Grayling, MI"
Catharine 1875 - 11 Dec
1941 C
PIERCHALSKI, Rozalia 4
Sept 18-- (illegible) - 30
Aug 1926 D
John 1879 - 11 Feb 1963 D
K 1906 - 1923 D
Mary 1880 - 3 Oct 1943 D
Franciszek dates illegible
D
PIERZYNSKI, Mary 8 Dec
1885 - 7 Nov 1912 E (Nee:
Gnoth) "First wife of John

PIERZYNSKI (continued)
J Pierzynski"
John J 1885 - 7 Jan 1964 E
Stella M 15 Oct 1890 - 14
Oct 1979 E (Nee: Hudak)
PIERZYNSKI, Frances 1861
mother - 1937 E (Nee:
Piasecki)
Stanley 1859 father - 1901
E
PIETERS, Freda 1878 - 24
Mar 1957 F
Theophilia 1870 - 26 Mar
1953
PIETRAZEWSKI (alias PE-
TERS), Marcin 1868 father
- 3 Jan 1947 C
Marya 1875 mother - 22
Dec 1963 C
Walerya -no dates- C
PIETRASZEWSKI, Mary -no
dates- D
Michael father -no dates- D
Frances mother -no dates-
D
PIETRZAK, Antony 1859 fa-
ther - 1933 C
Stella 1861 mother - 1934 C
(Nee: Wieczorek)
PIETRZAK, Petronella 1865
- 16 Mar 1939 H "Wife of
John Pietrzak" (Theofilia
Makowski Wincek & Jozef
Makowski same lot)
PILARSKI, Matthew 1885
father - 1932 C
Apolonia 1863 mother - 8
Apr 1948 C (Nee: Las-
kowski)
Henry 1899 son - 1903 C
PILARSKI, Anna 1893 - 15
Feb 1956 F
PILGER, Frank 1868 - 29
June 1947 -
PINKOWSKI, Josephine 19
July 1870 mother - 6 Aug

PINKOWSKI (continued)
1926 D (Nee: Kwilinski)
Ignatius 29 Sept 1865 father
- 22 June 1933 D
PINTER, William 1902 - 20
Aug 1939 H
Elizabeth 1862 - 24 Dec
1945 H "Died at Battle
Creek, MI"
PINTER, Geprge 1877 - 11
Dec 1951 C
PLAKE, Hattie 1891 - 4 June
1939 F
PLENCNER, Jadwiga 1874 -
16 June 1957 E (Nee:
Zalas)
Wojciech 1863 - 15 Dec
1930 E
Eliuguisz 1906 - 23 June
1946 E
PLOCKI-PIASECKI, Anna
1893 mother - 1956 F
(Joseph, Agnes, & Antony
Piasecki same lot)
PODELL, Joseph 1898 - 26
Jan 1958 D
PODELWITZ, Augustine
1871 father - 1915 A
Frances Radlicki 1878 mo-
ther - 25 Aug 1945 A (Nee:
Kowalski)
PODELWITZ, John 18 July
1842 - 21 July 1918 A
Julia 14 Feb 1846 wife -
19-- A
PODELWITZ, Frank 1868 -
1916 C
Valaria 1878 - 3 Jan 1964 C
(Nee: Makowski)
PODELWITZ, John 3 May
1870 - 13 Nov 1921 D
"Married to Kitty La Grue"
POKLINKOWSKI, John 1916
- 1917 C
M 1858 mother - 1936 C
Hattie 1885 - 16 Mar 1945

POKLONKOWSKI (continued)
C
Victor 1884 - 1962 C
POLICINSKI, Adeline S 1914
- no date C (Marcin &
Napomucena Ogniszak
same lot)
POORE, Ida 1874 - 1 Nov
1945 A
POPIELSKI, Rose 1858 mo-
ther - 1914 A (Nee: Ku-
jawski)
Michael K 1860 father -
1945 A
Henrietta 1903 wife - 1973
A
Adeline 1925 grand-
daughter - 2 Sept 1938 A
POWERS, Pat J 1870 - 9
June 1943 B "Died at Ber-
rien Springs, MI
POZGAI, R 1905 - 16 Apr
1954 A
PRALET, C 1895 - 13 Sept
1955 E
PRAWAT, Hattie 1892 -
1919 C
Edward 1901 - 1918 C
Antoni 1898 - 1916 C
Rozalia 1860 - 1916 C
"Wife of John Prawat,
nee: Zaworski"
Bronislawa 1889 - 1901 C
PRAWAT, Apolonia 1827 -
1907 D "Wife of William
Prawat"
PREUSS, Bruno ? - 8 Oct
1948 D
Theophilia 1888 - 12 June
1951 D
Frank J 1887 - 30 July 1966
D
E E 1926 - 20 June 1940 D
Lucille 1923 - 26 June 1940
D
PROBST, Rose 1896 - 14

PROBST (continued)
Dec 1961 F
Edmund A 1899 - 29 Mar
1966 F
Frances 1902 - 1 July 1967
F "Died in White Pigeon,
MI"
PROBST, Cynthia 1864 - 19
Aug 1938 C
Henry 1864 - 3 June 1941 C
PRZERADSKI, John 1869 -
17 Oct 1941 E
PRZESTWOR, Balzar 1852
father - 1909 C
Katharyn 1842 mother -
1925 C
John 1881 - 12 Apr 1956 C
(Joseph Spychalski same
lot)
PRZESTWOR, Jan 1866 hus-
band - 1905 C
Michalena 1873 wife - 1928
C
PRZESTWOR, Isabelle 1895
- 30 Mar 1963 E (Nee:
Campbell)
Stanley J 1888 - 7 July
1981 E
PRZYBYLINSKI, John Sr -no
dates- C
Helen -no dates- C (Nee:
Kujawski)
PRZYBYLINSKI, John Jr b &
d 1924 "Son of John Sr &
Helen Przybylinski" (Mar-
tin & Antonette Kujawski;
& E & S Tajkowski same
lot)
PRZYBYLINSKI, Valentyna
1875 - 1901 C (Nee: Zie-
linski) "Third Wife of
Michael Przybylinski"
Stanislawa 1863 - 1900 C
(Nee: Horka) "Second Wife
of Michael Przybylinski"
PRZYBYLINSKI, John 1868

PRZYBYLINSKI (continued)
father - 1932 E
Apolonia 1872 mother - 22
Jan 1967 E "Died at
Chicago, IL"
PRZYBYLISKI, Michal 1877
- 1935 F (Ignatius Lagocki
same lot)
PRZYBYSZ, Catharine 1877
- 31 Aug 1906 - (Nee:
Ciesielski)
PRZYBYSZ, Anzelm W 1890
husband - 1931 A
Veronica 1887 wife - 20
Aug 1960 A (Nee: Wituc-
ki)
Monika 1919 - 1920 A
Mary 1893 - 1894 A
no name 1867 mother -
1908 A
Aloysius F 10 Nov 1894
husband - 1932 A
Constance 1889 wife - 1
Dec 1962 A (Nee: Wituc-
ki) (Helen Witucki same
lot)
PRZYBYSZ, Wanda 1880 -
1977 B (Nee: Kowalek)
Stephen A 19 Apr 1882 - 28
May 1963 B
Eugene S 1910 - 27 Apr
1960 B
PRZYBYSZ, Helen V 1914 -
20 Oct 1946 D
Helen 1895 - 31 Oct 1963 D
(Nee: Klajbor)
Witold 1888 - 1924 D
Freda 1916 - 1935 D
PRZYBYSZ, Jozef 1854
father - 1931 D
Walerya 1859 mother -
1911 D (Nee: Mnichow-
ski)
Boleslaw 31 Aug 1880 - 11
Feb 1911 D
PRZYBYSZ, Martin 1856

PRZYBYSZ (continued)
Father - 1897 F
Magdelene 1863 mother -
1917 F (Nee: Chudzicki)
Valentine 1895 son - 1912
F
Katharine 1884 daughter -
1904 F
PRZYGOCKI, Teresa 1889 -
1973 A
Felix 1882 - 26 July 1972 A
(Eleanor Kolczynski &
Katarzyna Rychlewski
same lot)
PULASKI, Prakseda 1876 -
1937 C (Nee: Palicki)
Jan 1873 - 1919 C
Paul 23 July 1902 - 31 Aug
1962 C "IN Pfc 75 Eng Grp
WWII" (Stanislawa &
Wilhemina Palicki same
lot)
PURZYCKI, Joseph 1875 fa-
ther - 1926 D
Lottie 1875 mother - 24
Dec 1959 D
PUTASSKA, Mary 1874
mother - 1951 C
PUTZ, Frank S 1876 - 28 Apr
1947 C
Anna 1849 - 1924 C
Michael 1880 - 1919 C
Augustine 1881 - 1902 C
Stanley J 1890 - 1927 WWI
C
PUTZ, Joanna 1868 wife - 1
Apr 1946 D
Joseph 1891 son - no date
D (Andrew Wojciechowski
same lot)
PUTZ, Daniel J 1897 - 19
Aug 1967 D
PYSZKA, Marya 1852 - 1926
D
QUINLAN, J 1887 - 21 Jan
1955 Community Cemetery

QUINLAN (continued)
ND
QUINN, Katharyn 1880 - 24
Feb 1948 D "Died at La
Porte, IN"
Hugh -no dates- D "Died at
Walkerton, IN"
Marie L 1900 - 20 Oct 1970
D
RAAB, Catharine 1883 - 21
Sept 1960 A
John 1876 - 13 Jan 1950 A
RACZYNSKI, Bertha 1876 -
24 Mar 1962 A
Joseph 5 Sept 1873 - 26 Apr
1956 A "Pvt Co H 2 Regt
IL Inf Spanish American
War"
RACZYNSKI, Mary 1849 -
1908 A
Joseph 1805 - 1909 A
(Stanley, Julia, & Eligius
Nowak same lot)
RADAJ, Marya 1881 - 1900 C
(Wojciech, Frances, &
Stanislaw Maruszewski
same lot)
RADECKI, Jan no date - 10
Oct 1942 E
Katharine 1879 - 11 Jan
1966 E
RADICAN, Catharine E 1867
- 25 Mar 1950 A
John Patrick 1859 - 12 June
1949 A
RADKOVICH, Frank 1879 -
1928 D
Dorothy A 1925 - 2 May
1939 D
Bobby R 1928 - 1929 D
RADLICKI, Frances Podel-
witz 1878 - 24 Aug 1945 A
(Nee: Kowalski) (Augus-
tine Podelwitz same lot)
RADLICKI, Mary 1889
mother - 1917 - (Nee:

RADLICKI (continued)
Kowalski)
Stanley 1892 father - 1935 -
RADOMSKI, Telesfor S 1891
- 1978 C
Amelia 1889 - 20 Mar 1939
C (Nee: Otolski) "First
Husband: Joseph Smucin-
ski) (Michael L & Eleanor
Otolski; & Joseph & Blon-
dine Smucinski same lot)
RADZESZEWSKI, Clemen-
tine Niedbalski 1902 Gold
Star Mother - 14 Aug 1964
- (Leonard & Sylvester
Niedbalski same lot)
RAFINSKI, Anna 1860 - 1892
D
Francis 1856 - 1888 D
Joseph 1880 - 1881 D (Alo-
ysuis Smogor same lot)
RAFINSKI, Wladyslaw 1881
- 26 June 1949 D
Bronislawa 1882 - 13 Apr
1972 D
Gertrude 1919 - 1922 D
Edward 1919 - 1937 D
Genowefa 1900 - 1919 D
RAJDER, Frank 1876 - 1907
D (Josephine Sobczak
same lot)
RAJSKI, Anna 1869 - 13 Aug
1911 F (Nee: Jagla)
Catharine 1894 - 18 Sept
1961 F (Nee: Janowski)
(Bertha Szlanfucht same
lot)
RAJSKI, Piotr 5 Oct 1873 -
13 Feb 1898 F
John 1863 father - 1912 F
Antonina 1866 mother -
1933 F
Lena 1891 - 1916 F
William H 1885 - 19-- F
Klemenc 1911 son - 1933 F
Mary T 1885 mother - 1

RAJSKI (continued)
Nov 1967 F
Ignatius 1878 father - 4
Sept 1941 F
Daniel 1918 son - 1932 F
Virginia 1922 daughter -
1924 F
RAJSKI also RAYSKI, Joseph
V 1891 father - 22 Nov
1958 F (Michael & Joanna
Janowski same lot)
RAJTER, Michael 1888 -
1977 F "Pvt US Army
WWI"
Antoni 1884 - 1909 F
Wladyslaw 1880 - 1900 F
Jan 1875 - 1898 F
Antonina 1877 - 1895 F
no name 1822 grandmother
- 1906 F
Andrew 1841 father - 1909
F
Konstancia 1850 mother -
1915 F (K Bednorowicz
same lot)
READING, Maude 1874 - 17
Apr 1949 B
REDLING, Helen -no dates-
E
Mary -no dates- E
John -no dates- E (no name
Zgodzinski; Bert &
Josephine Magiera; S Dean
Dombkiewicz; & Hen-
rietta Woltman same lot)
REDMOND, John 1869 - 16
Sept 1939 A
James 1863 - 14 Apr 1942
A
REGIS, Roy 1877 - 14 Jan
1962 D
REHA, Joseph 1904 - no
date C
Frank 1881 - 19-- C
REICHANATER, Lucy 1856
- 1 May 1948 D

REIDER, Margaret 1874 - 7 Mar 1963 A
Conrad 1865 - 20 Apr 1939 A
Marie 1 Oct 1912 - 19 Oct 1912 A (Mamie Kroll same lot)
REITER, Thomas 10 days old - 16 Jan 1939 C
David Martnel 1901 - 1915 C
Joseph A 1872 - 1941 C
Kristen 1 day old - 28 Oct 1964 C
REMERY, Angela 1893 - 20 July 1965 F
Elizabeth 1870 - 22 Apr 1948 F
RENAUD, Theodore 1899 - 15 Aug 1960 E
REPCZYNSKI, Antonina no date - 1903 F (Nee: Bonat)
Antonette 1883 mother - 1916 F (Nee: Pinkowski)
Gustav 9 Apr 1854 - 1929 F
REPCZYNSKI, Alexander 1892 father - 1928 D
Alexander Jr 1928 - 10 May 1960 D
Valentina 1889 mother - 1 May 1970 D (Nee: Kujawski) "Daughter of Martin & Antonette Kujawski)
RHODES, Alfred J 1891 - 3 Nov 1969 -
RHODES, Henry J 1921 - 21 July 1948 C
Mary 1895 - 3 July 1960 C
RHODES, Elizabeth 1881 - 23 Oct 1957 D
RICHARDSON, Charles 1911 - 17 Apr 1941 A
RIDER, W 1881 - 18 Oct 1954 A
Martha 1884 - 12 Feb 1958 A

RIDER, Jacob -no dates- D
RIFFEL, Isaac 1875 - 29 May 1968 ?
RILEY, Phillip H no date - 5 Nov 1950 B
RITTER, Judith G 1916 - 24 Nov 1970 -
Harvey D 1904 - 18 Feb 1971 -
ROEMER, Wm F 1894 - 25 Sept 1971 C
J 1953 - 21 Aug 1955 C
M 4 hours old - 6 July 1956 C
ROGOZKA, Marcin 1845 - 19-- D
Joanna 1863 - 1892 D
ROKOP, Louis 1882 - 18 Aug 1962 D
Louis 1885 - 10 Sept 1951 D
ROKOP, Rose 1895 - 20 Mar 1970 - "Died at St Joseph, MI"
ROKOP, Andrew 1896 - 17 July 1946 A
ROMECKI, W no date - 1906 H
ROMSICKI, Stanley R 8 Feb 1905 - 16 Nov 1967 D
Leo 12 May 1896 - 23 July 1952 D "Pvt IN Co A 170 Eng WWI"
John 11 May 1887 - 30 Mar 1943 D "IN Pfc 22 Eng WWI" "Children of John & Victoria Romsicki"
ROMSICKI, Joseph no date - 27 Mar 1886 D (Peter & Mary M Chodzinski same lot)
ROMSICKI, John 1889 - 30 Mar 1943 F
John 11 Oct 1861 father - 11 July 1939 F
Victoria 18 Dec 1858 - 5

ROMSICKI (continued)
Mar 1925 F (Nee: Niez-
godski)
Rev Stephen G 18 Mar 1894
- 30 Aug 1942 F "Or-
dained 24 June 1922 -
Labored in Diocese of
Winona, MN 1923 to 1942
- Died at Sterling, MI"
(Helen & Jacob Wozniak
same lot)
ROSINSKI, Franciszka 1868 -
1906 C
"ROSHINSKE", Mike 25 Oct
1899 - 21 Oct 1954 C "IN
T/Sgt 450 Base Unit
WWII"
Henrietta 1908 - 1937 C
Jakob 1872 - 27 Jan 1958 C
ROSPLOCHOWSKI, Clara H
1898 - 1973 E (Nee: Clay-
ton)
John F 1875 - 4 Nov 1944 E
Esther 24 Aug 1902 - 24
Sept 1968 E
Clara 1867 - 25 Mar 1949 E
ROYTEK, Michalena 1875 -
22 June 1949 F (Nee: Lis-
zewski) (Jacob Tuligowski
same lot)
ROZANSKI, Wladyslaw 1870
- 1906 H
ROZEWICZ, Domika 1901 -
7 Apr 1970 -
ROZEWICZ, Margaret 1895 -
3 Mar 1944 A
ROZEWICZ, Joseph 1864 -
19 July 1943 C
ROZEWICZ, Tekla 1896 -
1907 G
Pawel 1858 father - 1919 G
Franciszka 1864 mother -
17 Nov 1938 G (Nee: Jan-
kowski)
Ceasor J 27 Aug 1895 - 26
July 1945 G "IN Pfc 3

ROZEWICZ (continued)
Motor Mech Regt Sig
Corps; died at Marion, IN"
ROZEWICZ, "Children" no
names -no dates- D
ROZEWICZ, Mary Ciegielski
1893 - 1934 E "Wife of
Peter Rozewicz" (Michael
& Sophie Ciegielski same
lot)
ROZEWICZ, Hubert 1855 -
1918 A
Pawel 1893 - 1916 A
Tekla -no dates- mother A
John -no dates- father A
RUDASICS, Elizabeth 1876 -
23 Sept 1949 D
RUDYNSKI, Mary 1852 mo-
ther - 1935 E (Nee:
Ciesiolka)
Anton 1851 father - 1921 E
RUDYNSKI, Leo H 1886 - 18
June 1966 E
Eleanor 1890 - 20 May 1947
E (Nee: Ciesiolka)
RUPEL, Edmund D 1922 - 30
May 1964 A "Died at Den-
ver, CO"
Mary J 1881 - 10 Mar 1969
A
Alex 1877 - 15 Dec 1941 A
RUSZKOWSKI, Mamie 1893
- 1921 E (Nee: Chrobot)
"Wife of Czeslaw Rusz-
kowski"
S 1904 - 27 May 1956 E
Catharine 1883 - 27 May
1941 E
RUSZKOWSKI, Maryanna
1865 mother - 1902 E
(Nee: Grzezinski)
Antony 1864 father - 13
June 1952 E
Steve 1901 - 1956 E
Stefan S 1928 son - 1931 E
RUSZKOWSKI, Theresa 1896

RUSZKOWSKI (continued)
daughter - 1962 F
Ladyslaw 1903 Son - 1936
F
Anna 1869 mother - 19 July
1947 F (Nee: Szybowicz)
Luke 1865 father - 1933 F
Casimir 1897 son - 1917 F
RUTKOWSKI, Michael 1853
- 6 Nov 1938 B
Josephine 1863 - 1928 B
(Nee: Makielski) (Tha-
deusz Janowiak; no name
Makielski; John & Jose-
phine Saberniak same lot)
RYAN, M 1870 - 15 Mar 1954
A
RYAN, Margaret 1871 - 13
July 1946 B
RYBARKIEWICZ, Walenty
1887 - 1901 E
Franciszek -no dates- E
Jozef -no dates- E
Wladyslaw -no dates- E
Katarzyna no dates- E
Anna -no dates- E
RYBECKI, Franciszek 1816 -
1903 C (Leonard Be-
czkiewicz same lot)
RYBICKI, Wladyslaw 1866
father - 30 Apr 1951 F
Wladyslaw 1885 - 1901 F
Franciszka 1870 mother -
1918 F (Nee: Rozplo-
chowski)
no name 1825 mother -
1911 F
no name 1825 father - 1904
F
Weronika 1892 - 1896 F
Edward 1894 - 1895 F
Benigna 1904 - 22 Nov 1962
F
RYCHLEWSKI, Katarzyna
1831 - 1915 A (Elanor
Kolczynski; & Felik &

RYCHLEWSKI (continued)
Teresa Przygocki same
lot)
RYDZINSKI, Maryanna 1860
- 1921 E
Franciszek 1862 - 1915 E
Stanislaw 1894 - 1903 E
Veronica 1896 - 3 Feb 1978
E
SABERNIAK, John 1891 - 4
Feb 1942 B
Josephine 1892 - 4 Feb
1947 B (Nee: Makielski)
(Tadeusz Janowiak; no
name Makielski; Michal &
Joephine Rutkowski same
lot)
SABERNIAK, Martin 4 Nov
1854 - 25 Dec 1905 C
Martin Jr 1907 - 1915 C
Anna 1884 - 1914 C
Augusta 1858 mother - 1929
C (Nee: Grams)
SALAMON, Rose 1889 - 16
Dec 1972 C
Paul 1882 - 9 Aug 1968 C
SALAMON, N 1870 - 2 July
1954 C
SALAMON, Bernard 1883 - 5
Feb 1948 D
Marie 1888 - 21 July 1942
D
SALLOWS, Edw H 1905 - 3
July 1970 C
Mary 1878 10 Jan 1963 C
SALLOWS, J 1903 - 10 Mar
1957 D
SARDI, Alex 1888 - 11 June
1958 H
SAUER, Frank 1885 - 1918 C
Stephen b 15 Feb 1909 C
John b 17 Feb 1911 C
Anna b 21 June 1917 C
SCHEETZ, Joseph M 1875 -
27 July 1945 A
SCHEIBELHUT, Lea 1891 -

SCHEIBELHUT (continued)
30 Jan 1971 -
SCHEIBELHUT, Peter 1865
- 30 Jan 1946 C
Rose 1863 - 19 Nov 1946 C
SCHEICBLHOFER, Elizabeth 1862 - 4 May 1944 D
SCHLINGERMAN, Catharine
1884 - 29 Sept 1969 -
SCHMIDT, M 1876 - 24 Aug
1955 H
Frances 1878 - 21 Aug 1966
H
J 1878 - 10 June 1956 H
SCHMIDT, E 1879 - 6 Dec
1953 F
SCHMIDT, A 1877 - 1 Aug
1954 A
SCHNEIDER, Mary 1883 - 14
Aug 1958 D
SCHREINER, A 1877 - 15
Oct 1954 E
SCHREYER, Elizabeth 1883
- 26 Mar 1971 D
Martin 1876 - 30 Aug 1961
D
SCHULER, Mamie 1880 - 20
Mar 1964 D
SCHULER, Mary 1864 - 29
Mar 1946 C
SCHULTZ, Robert Joseph 30
Dec 1894 - 11 Apr 1961 A
"IN C Smith 2 US Navy
WWI"
Augusta 1872 - 28 Oct 1957
A
SCHULTZ, Martha 1877 - 9
Apr 1946 F
SCHUMACHER, Rose 1888
- 26 Mar 1971 B
Frank J 1871 - 5 Oct 1964
B "Died at Tulsa, OK"
Julianna 1893 - 18 May
1967 B "Died at San Francisco, CA"
SCHUMACHER, Otto 1886 -

SCHUMACHER (continued)
19 May 1945 C "Died at
Chicago, IL"
Elizabeth 1854 - 12 Jan
1949 C
SCHUMACHER, B 1882 - 12
Nov 1954 A
SCHUSTER, John P 1907 - 2
Mar 1973 - "Died at
Marion, IN"
SCHUSTER, M 1867 - 12
June 1956 C
Katharine 1869 - 25 June
1949 C
SCIPSKI, Frank -no dates- D
Mary -no dates- D
SCOTT, J 1864 - 1 Jan 1955
B
Elizabeth M 1865 - 1 Feb
1950 B
SEGETY, Frank 1895 - 24
Jan 1958 F
Agatha Balog 1869 - 24
June 1948 F
SEHELSKI, no name -no
dates- F
SEIFERT, Anna 1883 - 21
Mar 1969 -
SEIFERT, A 1879 - 15 Oct
1941 C
Wm J 1868 - 9 Mar 1939 C
"Died at Tulsa, OK"
SEIFERT, Rose 1866 - 28
June 1943 F
SEISER, Christian 1875 - 23
Dec 1964 H
SELECKY, Theresa 1880 - 4
Jan 1955 C
Alexander 1880 - 1925 C
Helen 1908 - 1918 C
Grace 1906 - 28 Aug 1943 C
Ann 6 Oct 1910 - 30 July
1977 C
SENRICH, Mary 1871 - 7
June 1941 A
SENRICH, Frank 1869 - 1879

SENRICH (continued)
D
Mathilda 1873 - 1909 D
Magdelena 1843 - 1935 D
Frank A 1837 - 1894 D
SENRICH, J 1877 - 14 Apr
1957 H "Died at Chicago,
IL"
SHAFER, Margaret Winkler
1866 - 26 July 1951 A
Hiram 1861 - 30 Apr 1948 A
SHANK, Nettie 1886 - 23
Aug 1969 C
SHEEKEY, Molly 1876 - 21
Mar 1948 A
Joseph 1884 - 20 July 1942
A
SHERMAN, Michael 1872 -
8 Apr 1949 Community
Cemetery ND
SHOCK, F 1886 - 10 Mar
1956 B "Died at Niles,
MI"
SHROFF, Marlene S 12 Nov
1941 - 12 May 1975 C (So-
phie Dombrowski same
lot)
SIDERITS, Edward 1878 - 12
Feb 1962 G
Agnes 1894 - 13 June 1944
G
SIMON, Julia 1884 - 7 Apr
1964 H
Yves 1903 - 11 May 1961 H
SINGLER, Charles 1875 - 8
Feb 1946 A
SINKA, Theresa 1875 - 1
May 1946 D
Rokus 1877 - 7 Nov 1938 D
SINNOT, Agnes 1857 - 17
Apr 1942 C
SIPOTZ, Martha 1905 - 23
Mar 1960 C
Mary 1877 - 23 Oct 1949 C
Louis 1873 - 24 Dec 1946 C
SKARICH, Teresa 1885 - 19

SKARICH (continued)
July 1959 C "Wife of An-
ton Skarich"
SKARUPINSKI, Maryanna -no
dates- D
Franciszek -no dates- D
Anna -no dates- D
SKARUPINSKI, Konstancya
1877 - 18 Dec 1904 A
(Nee: Micinski)
John 9 Jan 1875 - 2 Mar
1948 A
Apolonia 1882 2nd Wife -
1926 A (Nee: Nejman)
SLANE, James R ? - 1931 F
(Jakob, Mary, & Henry P
Wawrzynczak same lot)
SLEDZIKOWSKI, Alex 1895
husband, father - 5 Sept
1959 B
Frances F 1898 wife, mo-
ther - 24 Mar 1945 B (Nee:
Chodzinski)
Maryanna 1870 wife, mother
- 13 Mar 1965 B (Nee:
Woodka)
Roman J 1867 father hus-
band - 1937 B (Stanislaw
& Stanislawa Mnichowski
same lot)
SLISZ, Marya 10 Mar 1857 -
9 Feb 1896 F "First Wife
of Anton Slisz, nee: Stetz"
Michael 9 Sept 1886 - 24
May 1902 F
Balbina 10 Mar 1857 - 29
Nov 1910 F (Nee: Las-
kowski) "First Wife of
Walter Goraczewski,
Second Wife of Anton
Slisz"
Teodozia 29 May 1900 - 6
Apr 1902 F
SLOTT, Elizabeth C 1876
mother - 15 Oct 1946 C
(Nee: Gorski)

SLOTT (continued)
Henry G 1870 father - 1940
C
Cecylia 1909 daughter -
19-- C
SLOTT, Rose Fay 1874 - 27
July 1951 E (Nee: Koma-
sinski)
Martin J 1869 - 10 Feb
1947 E
Henry 1880 - 12 Nov 1940 E
(Sophie G Trzcinski same
lot)
SMIGIELSKI, Klemenc 1856
- 1906 E
Antonina -no dates- E
Stanislaw -no dates- E
Antoni -no dates- E
Jozefa -no dates- E
Franciszek -no dates- E
SMITH, Barbara 1867 - 5
June 1945 A
Mary E 1864 - 29 Apr 1939
A
SMITH, Anna 1886 - 25 Jan
1941 A
SMITH, Helena 1871 - 11
Feb 1950 C
Peter 1875 - 30 May 1946 C
"Died at Chicago, IL"
SMITH, Marie 1910 - 30 Oct
1940 C
SMITH, Johanna 1855 - 19
Jul 1943 F "Died at
Wayne County, MI"
SMOGOR, Clement 1876 -
1924 A
Mary B 1877 - 9 June 1953
A (Nee: Rafinski)
SMOGOR, Aloysius 1901 -
1901 D (Francis & Anna
Rafinski same lot)
SMOGOR, Maryanna 1849 -
1923 C
Antoni 1844 - 1914 C (Mi-
chal Myszka same lot)

SMUCINSKI, Joseph 1887 -
1914 C
Blondine 1910 - 1929 C
(Michael L & Eleanora
Otolski; & Telesfor &
Amelia Radomski same
lot)
SMUDZINSKI, Jean 1916 - 6
Dec 1972 -
SNIADECKI, Erwin J 1917 -
1930 D
Louis 1894 - 29 Nov 1958 D
Bernice 1892 - 22 Nov 1968
D
Aniella 1895 - 1926 D (Nee:
Nowak)
SOBCZAK, Jadwiga Kurek 22
Oct 1884 - 19 Nov 1917 D
"Wife of Stanley Kurek"
Josephine 1854 mother - 24
Apr 1938 D (Nee: Herman)
(Frank Rajder same lot)
SOBIERALSKI, Leon 1902 -
1904 C
Jozef 1899 - 1901 C
Teodor 1863 father - 1935 C
Paulina 1870 mother - 1932
C
SOBIERALSKI, Alfred 1915 -
1924 E (Wladyslaw &
Maryanna Taberski; &
Leon, Frances, & Mary R
Bulmanski same lot)
SOJKA, Julianna 1881 - 1934
C
Antonina 1859 mother - 24
Oct 1930 C (Nee: Szy-
bowicz)
Joseph 1859 father - 1901 C
Anna 1892 - 27 Nov 1952 C
SOKOLICH, August 1883 fa-
ther - 1964 E (with pic-
ture)
August 1911 son - 1918 E
Terez 1885 mother - 1967 E
SOKOLOWSKI, Mary 1864 -

SOKOLOWSKI (continued)
15 Dec 1899 C "Husband:
Wojciech Skolowski in-
terred at St Joseph Polish
Cemetery"
SOLARI, Mary 1854 - 29 Sept
1943 -
SOLOMON, Rose A 1891 -
10 Jan 1944 E
SOLOMON, Helen 1881 - 6
Mar 1939 A
SOPCZYNSKI, John -no
dates- C
Leo 1883 - 20 Nov 1940 C
SOPCZYNSKI, Antonina 1867
mother - 15 Aug 1930 C
Franciszek 1863 father -
1936 C
Alex S 6 June 1891 - 27
Sept 1957 C "IN Pfc 329
Baker Co QMC WWI"
SOPCZYNSKI, Jozef 1878 -
1906 A
Jan 1832 - 1913 A
Anna 1833 - 1916 A (Jan &
Eleanor Wroblewski same
lot)
SOSINSKI, Stanislaw 1897 -
1931 E
Wladyslaw 1878 - 1913 E
Frances 1859 mother - 1928
E (Nee: Krieger)
John 1845 father - 1911 E
Genowefa 6 months old -
1900 E
Pelegia 1893 - 1903 E
(Florentyna Wenslaw
same lot)
SOSNOWSKI, Jadwiga -no
dates- D
Maryanna -no dates- D
Albina -no dates- D
Zygmund -no dates- D
Rozalia 4 Sept 1846 mother
- 23 July 1913 D
Ignacy 13 July 1844 father -

SOSNOWSKI (continued)
27 Aug 1910 D
SOWALA, Lawrence 1892 -
1920 E (Ladyslaw & Mary
Kruk; Richard Daniel
Cook; & Stephan K Gish
same lot)
SOWELL, T 1879 - 30 Jan
1957 C
SPERLINSKI, no name 1915
sister - 1916 A
no name 1840 grandfather -
1920 A
Max 1871 father - 11 Apr
1958 A
Martha 1877 mother - 6 Mar
1960 A
SPILLMAN, Bertha 1897 - 6
Apr 1939 C "Died at
Boulder City, NV"
SPLAWSKI, Janina 1891
daughter - 1917 C
(Maryanna & Wincenty
Gudajtys same lot)
SPYCHALSKI, Joseph 1874 -
17 Oct 1953 C (John
Przestwor same lot)
SPYCHALSKI, Frank J 3 Dec
1890 - 27 May 1946 E "IN
Sgt 362 Inf 91 Div WWI"
SPYCHALSKI, Salomea 1883
wife - 30 Sept 1957 C
(Nee: Daszynski)
Stephen 1875 husband - 3
May 1946 C
Andrzej -no dates- C
Agnieszka no date - 21 Dec
1925 C (Nee: Chole-
wczynski) (Constance
Nitka same lot)
STACHOWIAK, Maryanna
1851 mother - 1935 A
Marcin 1852 father - 1926 A
Rev Antony 5 May 1878 -
25 May 1925 A (Mary
Kasza same lot)

STACHOWIAK, Katarzyna 1834 mother - 17 Jan 1910 E

Agnes 1861 - 4 July 1903 E (Nee: Kujawski) "Wife of Bartholomew Stachowiak interred at St Joseph Polish Cemetery"

STACHOWIAK, Joseph 1885 - 18 Jan 1948 D

Regina C 1887 - 28 Oct 1970 D (Nee: Palicki) (Szymon & Konstancya Palicki; Joseph & Anna Wroblewski; & Bertha Miller same lot)

STACHOWIAK, Larry J 24 July 1891 - 31 Jan 1949 D

Nellie S 1893 - 8 July 1972 D (Nee: Janowski)

STACHOWIAK, John 1857 father - 8 Jan 1898 F

Katharine 25 July 1863 mother - 12 Jan 1942 F (Nee: Jarecki) (Bertha Stachowiak Allison same lot)

STACHOWSKI, Edwin J 27 May 1905 - 1 July 1944 F "IN Pvt 331 Inf 83 Div WWII"

Rozalea 1877 - 19 Jan 1967 F (Nee: Paryz)

Joseph 1872 - 4 Sept 1949 F

Edward 1908 - 25 May 1948 F

STACHOWSKI, Julius S 1902 - 1978 C "F 3 US Navy WWI"

STACHOWICZ, John F 1878 - 9 Apr 1944 E

Pelegia 1874 - 16 Dec 1952 E

STAJKOWSKI, Jan 1871 father - 1936 E

STAJKOWSKI (continued) Maryanna 1876 mother - 15 Dec 1957 E

STARCZEWSKI, Walenty 1887 - 1929 F

John 1855 - 1916 F

Josephine 1874 - 1924 F

STASIAK, Jacob 1852 - 1913 C

Maryanna no date - 13 Aug 1908 C (Rose Gonsiorowski same lot)

STEFFELEN, F 1905 - 28 June 1955 C

STEFINSKI, Max 28 Jan 1881 - 2 Jan 1936 C

Mary 1856 - 23 July 1941 C

Valentine 1861 - 4 May 1938 C

STEMPIN, Lottie mother - no dates- B

Harry son -no dates- B

Mary 1891 - 29 June 1960 B

Paul Klezle 1919 - 1921 B

STEMPIN, Joseph 1882 - 23 Nov 1969 E (Antoni & Antonina Marcinkowski same lot)

STERNBURGH, Charles 1851 - 23 Feb 1941 E

STEVENS, B 1901 - 22 May 1956 H "Died at Oak Park, IL"

STEYAERT, Victor 1886 - 28 Nov 1951 B

STEYAERT, Irma 1886 - 1 Apr 1961 C

STOCKINGER, J 1864 - 29 Aug 1955 A

STONEY, C 1867 - 9 Nov 1956 D

STOREY, James R 1897 - 2 Aug 1970 -

STOREY, Mary Rose 1903 - 18 Sept 1967 C

STRANTZ, Barbara 1896 - 4

STRANTZ (continued)
Apr 1973 F
Stephen 1890 - 25 July 1968
F
STRANTZ, Frances 1862
mother - 1925 B (John J &
Mary Kieran same lot)
STRANTZ, Elizabeth 1875
mother - 24 June 1964 C
(Nee: Tschida)
Leopold 1870 father - 1916
C
Leo 1903 son - 6 Apr 1945
C
Katarzyna 1913 daughter -
10 Sept 1966 C
STRANTZ, Victor 13 May
1880 husband - 2 Oct 1945
C
Josephine 16 Sept 1880 wife
- 31 Dec 1963 C
STRANTZ, Jozef 1849 father
- 1927 C
Rozalia 1849 mother - 1905
C (Nee: Rosiech)
STRANTZ, Joseph 28 Apr
1904 son - 5 May 1939 C
Theresa E 22 May 1869
mother - 12 Apr 1941 C
(Nee: Curtis)
Michael G 29 May 1868
father - 14 Sept 1937 C
Paul 8 Mar 1906 - 14 Sept
1920 C
Julianna 11 Apr 1831 - 22
Jan 1908 C
STRANTZ, Michael M 1895 -
20 July 1940 D "IN Cpl
129 Guard Co"
William S 1893 - 24 Dec
1939 D "IN Pvt US Army"
Theresa 1902 - 28 Sept
1972 D
STROHMAYER, Leopold
1867 - 6 May 1941 C
STROHMEYER, Katharine

STROHMEYER (continued)
1877 - 22 May 1939 G
STROPKA, Mary 1887 - 1974
B
Zigmond 1881 father - 15
July 1956 B
STROPKA, Gizella 1889 -
1918 A
STRUCK, Jan 1840 - 1913 C
Franciszka 1843 - 1925 C
(Steven & Amelia Lasecki;
& Cecelia Broyles same
lot)
STULTS, Genevieve V 1896 -
1928 F (Nee: Szczechow-
ski) (Anna, Peter Paul, &
Karolny Szczechowski
same lot)
STYPCZYNSKI, Pawel -no
dates- C
Ludwika -no dates- C
Ferdynand -no dates- C
SULLIVAN, Anna Loretta
1909 - 8 Jan 1969 - "Died
at Benton Harbor, MI"
SULLIVAN, Josephine 1899 -
14 Oct 1970 - "Died at
Tucson, AZ"
SULLIVAN, Mary M 1916 -
12 Dec 1971 B
Anna 1885 - 13 Nov 1962 B
"Both died at Benton Har-
bor, MI"
SULLIVAN, Mary 1871 - 21
Mar 1967 A
Katharyn L 1881 - 1 May
1950 A
Lloyd 1898 - 22 Dec 1958 A
SULLIVAN, Ida 1853 - 16
Feb 1940 D "Died at Chi-
cago, IL"
SUMPTION, George 1886 -
22 Nov 1968 - "Died at In-
dianapolis, IN"
SUMPTION, Agnes 1890 - 25
Oct 1963 C

SUPERCZYNSKI, Eleanora 1889 - 16 June 1969 D (Paul & Anna Grega same lot)
SUPERCZYNSKI, Michaline 1860 mother - 1930 E
Hattie 1890 - 15 Oct 1956 E (Lottie & Walter Szulczewski same lot)
SUTH, Anna K 1880 - 21 Dec 1942 -
SUTH, Alex K 1922 - 11 Mar 1949 E
SWANK, Mary 1885 - 7 Feb 1960 D
Mary 1936 - 19 Apr 1943 D
Ruth Anna 1938 - 10 May 1973 D
SWIATOWY, Edward J infant - 1922 E
Joseph F 1859 father - 1925 E
SWINGENDORF, Fred P 1906 - 13 Aug 1969 -
SWINIARSKI, Julianna 1863 - 1891 D
Walenty 1856 - 2 June 1938 D
SWINSKI, Eleanor 1878 - 14 June 1959 H
SWINSKI, Leo B 1847 - 1935 A
Cecylia 1845 - 1902 A
SWITALSKI, Victoria 1849 mother - 1914 F
Joanna 1881 wife - 1960 F (Nee: Makowski)
Peter 1878 husband - 14 Aug 1942 F
SYNAVE, Mary 1887 - 24 Feb 1943 D
SYPNIEWSKI, Bronislawa 1852 mother - 1930 A
Anna B 1879 daughter - 1920 A
SZABO, Elizabeth 1909 - 10

SZABO (continued) Sept 1969 -
SZABO, Elizabeth 1901 - 17 Oct 1971 -
SZABO, Gaspar 1877 - 19 Jan 1958 -
SZABO, Mary 1873 - 11 June 1949 A
SZABO, Emery 1887 - 8 June 1966 B
Margaret 1872 - 8 July 1945 B
Joseph 1872 - 3 Dec 1951 B
SZABO, Mary Rose 1903 - 18 Sept 1967 C
SZABO, Menyhart 1873 - 2 June 1957 D
SZABO, Elizabeth 1868 - 21 May 1950 F
Mary 1873 - 11 June 1949 F
Charles 1900 - 1 Jan 1942 F
SZALAY, Anna 1887 - 24 May 1958 C
Geza 1869 - 9 Aug 1949 C
SZALAY, Mary 1889 - 19 Feb 1941 H
SZALEWSKI, Zygmunt 1899 - 1903 C
Janina 1898 - 1905 C
SZAMECKI, Frank 1888 husband - 6 Oct 1955 F
Wawrzyniec 1855 father - 1931 F
Franciszka 1859 mother - 1932 F (Nee: Stempierski)
Wladyslaw -no dates- F
Martha 1888 wife - 1974 F (Nee: Luzny)
SZAMECKI, Frank A 1879 - 11 Apr 1954 D "Died in Logansport, IN"
SZAMECKI, Edward C no date - 6 Aug 1930 D "Pvt SATC Indianapolis Cham-

71

SZAMECKI (continued)
ber of Commerce"
SZAMECKI, Alexander no
date - 16 Nov 1924 -
SZCZAPINSKI, Stanley F
1877 - 27 June 1965 A
Frances 1865 - 3 Dec 1938
A (Nee: Dominski) (Hen-
rietta Fill & Felix
Dominski same lot)
SZCZECHOWSKI, Anna 1875
- 24 Mar 1970 F (Nee:
Grabarz)
Peter Paul 1863 - 14 Nov
1950 F
Karolyn 1833 mother - 1898
F (Genevieve Szczechow-
ski Stults same lot)
SZCZECHOWSKI, no name -
no dates- C
SZCZESNIAK, Natalie 1915 -
22 Sept 1967 E
Prof Boleslaw 1908 - 19--
E
SZCZESNIAK, Andrew L 8
Oct 1938 - 31 Oct 1970 E
Leszek B 26 July 1935 - 20
Mar 1970 E "IN Sgt 17 Inf
Regt 7 Div"
SZCZYPIORSKI, Piotr 1860 -
1927 C (Stephen & An-
tonina Lewandowski same
lot)
SZENDREI, Ida 1877 - 3 July
1942 C
SZEWCZYK, Julia 14 Apr
1920 - 8 Oct 1920 D
(Edward & Rose Gramza
same lot)
SZLANFUCHT, Bertha 1887
mother - 1929 F (Nee:
Rajski) "Wife of Alex
Szlanfucht" (Anna & Cath-
arine Rajski same lot)
SZLANFUCHT, Jan 1881 -
12 June 1957 E

SZLANFUCHT (continued)
Walaria 1886 - 8 Feb 1965
E
Jozefa 1850 - 1937 E
Ludwig 1843 - 1903 E (Es-
tell Szlanfucht Krzy-
chowski same lot)
SZOKOL, Jozef 10 Aug 1915
- 13 Apr 1917 E
SZKOLICS, Theresa 1881 -
21 Mar 1969 C
August 1871 - 12 July 1951
C
SZOTYNSKI, Frank 9 Jan
1861 - 31 Oct 1947 D
SZULCZEWSKI, Antony 1857
- 1925 F
Stella 1861 - 1931 F
Mary 1890 - 7 Nov 1962 F
"Died at Detroit, MI"
SZULCZEWSKI, Lottie 25
Dec 1896 - 23 Sept 1971 E
Walter Frank 16 May 1892
- 10 Sept 1954 E "IN Pvt
Btry B 6 Regt WWI"
(Michalena & Hattie Su-
percinski same lot)
SZYBOWICZ, Helen 1893
daughter - 14 Feb 1958 D
Josephine 1852 mother -
1926 D (Nee: Rozek)
Antony S 1852 father - 1897
D
SZYBOWICZ, Frank 1828
father - 1912 A
Julia 1838 mother - 1921 A
(Nee: Drajus)
Anna 1873 - 1924 A
Mary 1876 - 1940 A
SZYBOWICZ, Joseph S 1879
- 1926 F
Mary 1880 - 19 Apr 1940 F
(Robert Patrick Allen
same lot)
SZYMANSKI, Emelia 30
June 1859 - 8 Dec 1936 A

SZYMANSKI (continued)
(Nee: Lesecki)
Wladyslaw 1857 - 1917 A
Sylvester A 1899 - 15 Sept
1966 A
SZYMANSKI, Aurelia 1896 -
20 Jan 1954 C
Ernest 1907 - 26 May 1922
C
Mary 1871 - 22 Nov 1957 C
(Nee: Andrysiak)
Antony 1871 - 16 Feb 1951
C
SZYMANSKI, John M 28 Aug
1889 husband - 22 Nov
1981 C
Anastasia M 1893 wife - 22
Sept 1964 C
SZYMANSKI, baby 1 day old
- 6 Mar 1943 E
SZYMANOWSKI, Alex -no
dates- D (Franciszek &
Agnieszka Zielinski same
lot)
SYMCZAK, Frank 5 Mar
1875 - 5 Apr 1942 F
Frances 29 Sept 1881 - 1
June 1965 F (Nee: Banach)
(Leo Banach same lot)
SZYMKOWIAK, Edmund
1912 - 24 Dec 1930 E
Frances 1904 - 26 Mar
1972 E
Mary 1877 - 21 May 1966 E
(Nee: Nowak)
Joseph 1864 - 1914 E
SZYMKOWIAK, Antoni 1865
father - 1932 E
Katarzyna 1867 mother - 1
July 1955 E (Nee: Chud-
zicki)
Stanislaw 1898 son - 1933
E
SZULCZYK, Michalena 1845
- 1902 C
Ignacy 1841 - 1914 C

TABACOFF, Richard 1923 -
23 Apr 1969 -
TABERSKI, Louis 1894 - 11
Aug 1950 E
Pelegia 1859 - 1926 E
Maryanna 1852 mother -
1917 E
Wladyslaw 1889 - 1914 E
Irene -no dates- E
Helen -no dates- E
Edmund -no dates- E
Henrietta -no dates- E
Renata -no dates- E
Henry -no dates- E
Roman 1881 - 1929 E (Le-
on, Franciszek, & Mary
Bulmanski same lot)
TAJKOWSKI, Edward J 1913
- 17 Apr 1971 A
Franciszek S 1880 - 3 Mar
1950 A
Kazimiera 1882 - 1919 A
(Nee: Niezgodski)
TAJKOWSKI, E 1915 - 1915
C
S 1917 - 1917 C (Martin &
Antonette Kujawski; &
John Przybylinski, Jr
same lot)
TAJKOWSKI, Wojciech 1847
- 1887 D "First Husband
of Antonette Laskowski
Tajkowski Kujawski"
TAKACS, Frank 1932 - 24
Aug 1952 G
Frank 1886 - 21 Feb 1946 G
TANSEY, Gwendolyn V 1897
- 19 Nov 1966 A
Mary Ann 1856 - 31 Aug
1944 A
TANS, Joseph 1909 - 16 Dec
1968 D
John 1894 - 28 Sept 1960 D
TAYLOR, Mary 1866 - 26
June 1943 E
TEZER, Catharine 1892 - 10

TEZER (continued)
Apr 1962 E
THELEN, Lulu 1875 - 4 May 1959 A
THILMAN, Alexander M 1892 father - 14 July 1967 B
Aurelia S 1892 mother - 1977 B
THILMAN, Joseph P 1879 father - 6 Nov 1951 C
John 1871 - 15 Apr 1947 C
Agnes -no dates- C
Elizabeth 1885 mother - 3 May 1973 C
THILMAN, Sylvester 1879 - 1935 D
Casimir 1886 - 1 Mar 1951 D
Floretyna 1857 mother - 1936 D
Leon 1854 father - 1893 D
THILMAN, Lillian C 16 Aug 1888 - 23 Apr 1967 D (Stanislaw & Anna Kolczynski same lot)
THOMAS, Anna 1881 - 1919 A (Nee: Arndt)
Ruth J 1915 - 13 Feb 1970 A
Mary 1884 - 5 Nov 1957 A (Harry J & Katharine Arndt same lot)
THOME, John James 1895 - 12 Oct 1966 D
THOMPSON, Frank 1892 - 11 Apr 1966 A
THOMPSON, Blanche 1888 - 18 Sept 1968 -
Gertrude no date - 26 Sept 1971 -
THORNE, Elizabeth 1875 - 30 Oct 1939 D
THORNTON, Leo 1895 - 24 Feb 1972 -
TOBOLSKI, William 1885

TOBOLSKI (continued)
father - 2 May 1969 C
Anna 1888 mother - 25 Sept 1968 C (Nee: Kowalski)
TOBOLSKI, Jacob 1853 father - 1888 D (Konstanty Kinowski same lot)
TOEPP, Margaret 1897 - 30 Oct 1938 A
Josephine 1861 - 30 Apr 1940 A "Both died at Kalamazoo, MI"
TOEPP, Josephine 1861 - 12 Apr 1947 C
TOMAJCZYK, Walenty 14 Feb 1822 - 9 Mar 1923 F
Katarzyna 1817 - 1900 F
TOMASI, Louis 1881 - 29 July 1950 C
Rose 1892 - 10 Aug 1972 C
TOMLINSON, Agnes 1875 - 4 Aug 1962 C
Albert M 1869 - 7 June 1947 C
TOMOLAK, Goldie 1876 - 29 July 1959 B
K 1875 - 26 Apr 1953 B
TONK, Frances 1880 - 18 Aug 1966 H
Frank 1878 - 19 Sept 1972 H
TOROK, Louis 1889 father - 10 Aug 1964 D
Theresa 1895 mother - 19-- D
Steve 1858 - 1922 D
TOROK, Rose 1875 mother - 1936 D
Gyorgy 1852 - 1920 D (Jozef Kaczmarek same lot)
TOROK, Agnes 1871 - 10 May 1964 G
Louis 1851 - 1915 G
John 1911 - 1911 G
TOROK, Agatha 21 Dec 1877 - 4 Mar 1945 A

TOROK (continued)
Joseph 19 Mar 1875 - 15 Nov 1918 A
Rosa 4 July 1900 - 17 Apr 1911 A
Joan Marie 1934 - 1937 A "Daughter of A & M Torok"
TORZEWSKI, John 1881 father - 1930 D
Lottie -no dates- mother D (Nee: Mazurkiewicz)
TORZEWSKI, Stanislawa -no dates- E
Genowefa 1919 - 1924 E
Eugeniusz 1925 - 1926 E
Magdelina 16 Nov 1857 mother - 1 Jan 1918 "Wife of Joseph Torzewski, nee: Rozanski"
TOTAR, Stephen 1876 - 26 Aug 1943 F
TOTH, George 1883 - 29 May 1967 A
Rose 1881 - 2 Apr 1956 A
TOTH, Regina 1891 - 27 Jan 1968 C "Died at Cincinnati, OH"
Joseph 1928 - 17 Aug 1962 C
Anna 1895 - 3 Mar 1946 C
John 1891 - 11 Nov 1959 C
TOTH, Helen 1880 - 27 Mar 1970 C
Joseph 1906 - 1 Apr 1959 C "Died at Washoe, NE"
Rose 1866 - 5 Feb 1950 C
TOTH, Joseph 1863 - 28 Mar 1941 E
TOUHEY, Tim 1882 - 28 July 1962 C
Katharine 1887 - 7 July 1939 C
Simon 1871 - 21 Sept 1939 C
TOUHEY, Mary 1856 - 2 Dec

TOUHEY (continued)
1946 B "Died at Chicago, IL"
TOWNSEND, M 1879 - 23 Jan 1955 B
TRIMMER, Mary 1893 - 18 Sept 1970 -
Matthew 1884 - 15 May 1948 -
TROK, Szymon 1847 - 2 Dec 1897 D
Antonina 19 Apr 1848 - 24 Aug 1917 D
Joseph F 28 Dec 1880 - 27 Mar 1935 D
TRUMBULL, Caroline 1881 - 9 Mar 1958 C
TRZCINA, John 1890 - 1974 F (Jan & Jawiga Witkowski, & John & Mary Wieczorek same lot)
TRZCINSKI, Sophie G 1895 - 4 May 1973 E (Rose Fay & Martin Slott same lot)
TSCHIDA, Mary 1875 - 9 Feb 1958 C
J 1878 - 20 Dec 1954 C
TSCHIDA, John 1869 - 19 Mar 1939 C
Anna 1879 - 31 Dec 1944 C
TSCHIDA, Frank 1900 - 28 Jan 1947 A
Katharine 1870 - 12 Aug 1940 A
TSCHIDA, Elizabeth 1850 - 16 Nov 1939 F
TUDOR, Emerence 1873 - 10 Nov 1964 C
Nicholas 1874 - 31 Jan 1944 C
TULIGOWSKI, Jakob 1870 - 1897 F (Michalina Roytek same lot)
TURNOCK, William 1885 - 22 Aug 1960 A
Mary 1886 - 24 Nov 1961 A

UERSELDEN, J 1910 - 25 Jan 1955 C

ULLERY, Clara J 1863 - 29 Mar 1947 A

URBANSKI, no name 12 Aug 1843 wife - 13 Mar 1906 F "Wife of Mikolaj Urban- ski"

URBANOWSKI, Jozef 1839 - 1907 F

Marcyanna 1813 - 1897 F

VAGA, S 1877 - 29 Nov 1953 B

VANDERHAEGEN, Elda 1861 - 9 Sept 1942 D

VANDERHOFF, Mary E 1886 - 16 May 1968 A "Died at Windsor, Canada"

VANHECK, Stefania 1880 - 15 Apr 1960 B

VANHOWE, Rosalie 1868 - 15 Mar 1946 C

VANLAECKE, Mary 1882 - 11 July 1964 C

Helen 1896 - 25 Feb 1966 C

VANLAECKE, Triphon 1873 - 13 Nov 1943 C

VANLAECKE, Julius 1885 - 15 Oct 1963 C

VANLAERE, Rene 1889 - 10 Dec 1969 -

VAN WINKLE, Harold 1905 - 1 Feb 1969 -

VARGA, Anna no date - 1 May 1946 A

V 1878 - 20 Apr 1954 A

George 1888 - 12 Apr 1965 A

Andrew 1902 - 14 Aug 1963 A

VARGA, Rose 1892 - 26 Feb 1969 -

Joseph 1887 - 28 Aug 1949 -

VARGA, Mary 1876 - 5 May 1958 B

VARGO, Theresa 1888 - 1 Jan 1947 C

VARGYAS, Joseph 1891 - 9 June 1967 D

Julia 1869 - 10 Apr 1941 D

Joseph 1905 - 24 Dec 1942 D

Vera 1885 - 2 Aug 1945 D

VASCIL, Julia 1878 - 11 June 1950 C "Wife of An- drew Vascil"

VASZARI, John 1884 - 16 Jan 1958 B

Regina 1885 - 14 Apr 1944 B

VAYDA, Daniel 1884 - 10 Oct 1968 -

VECS, Nicholas 1893 - 22 June 1962 H

Agnes 1891 - 16 Dec 1967 H

Mary 1861 - 8 June 1940 H

VENNET, Grace 1885 - 30 Jan 1943 A

VERCANTEREN, August 1861 - 16 Feb 1943 D

VERKA, Mary no date - 10 Mar 1941 A "Died at Den- ver, CO"

VERSELDER, Camiel 1882 - 13 Jan 1963 C

Louise 1887 - 6 Mar 1942 C

VILFLOR, P 1875 - 1 Feb 1955 Community Cemetery ND

VLERICK, Leon 1861 - 12 Mar 1951 F

VOELKERS, Gertrude 1905 - 22 Jan 1961 A

Regina 1867 - 20 July 1948 A "Died at Chicago, IL"

VOGG, C Bernie 1886 - 9 Mar 1939 E

VOLLMER, Anna E 1925 - 17 Mar 1947 A "Died at Evansville, IN"

VOLZER, Anna L 1880 - 7 Oct 1966 E
Clarence 1888 - 3 Mar 1959 E
VOORDE, Edward 1911 - 2 Sept 1960 F
Anna 1880 - 19 May 1957 F
VOORDE, Joseph 1879 - 20 Sept 1959 C
Rev D 1905 - 18 Nov 1954 C
VOORDE, Mary 1884 - 27 Dec 1968 -
David 1879 - 1 Jan 1969 -
VOSS, Louis 1880 - 21 Mar 1961 C
VOYNOVICH, G 1889 - 12 Mar 1957 D
Frederich 1922 - 22 July 1948 D
VUCKICS, Stephen 1893 - 26 Apr 1938 A
WAGEMAN, Ida 1867 - 8 Apr 1944 D "Died at Avilla, IN; wife of Edward Wageman"
WAGNER (See: WEGNER), Joseph 26 Nov 1899 - 11 Oct 1959 D "IN Pfc Army Air Force WWI" (Ludwig & Maryanna Wegner same lot)
WAHLEN, Lulu 1890 - 25 May 1972 -
WAHLEN, Anna 1861 - 6 Apr 1940 A
WAIT, Katharine 1896 - 30 Oct 1964 A
WAIT, Max 1882 - 7 Sept 1944 F
WALINSKI, William 1904 Son - 1904 C
Tillie 1876 mother - 4 Nov 1940 C
Frank J 1876 father - 9 Sept 1959 C

WALKER, Harry 1881 - 5 Dec 1943 D "Died at Anderson, IN"
WALKOWIAK, Frank 1865 - 25 July 1948 E
Magdeline 1868 - 4 Apr 1951 E
WALL, William F 1889 - 1 Jan 1969 -
WALLISCH, Frank J 1891 - 1918 F
Julia 1860 mother - 1919 F
John 1856 father - 1929 F
John F 1887 - 1949 F
Martianna 1893 - 1964 F
WALLISCH, Frank 1889 - 5 Oct 1952 C
WALSH, Edward 1889 - 9 Nov 1949 B
WALSH, Michael 1871 - 24 Apr 1948 -
WALSH, Eva no date - 20 Sept 1938 A
WALSH, George S 1889 - 18 Dec 1948 F
WALTER, Theresa 1859 mother - 1936 D
Julia M 1892 - 1924 D (Flora Poulin same lot)
WALZ, A 1887 - 8 Sept 1956 D
WARGIN, Walter 1875 - 28 July 1946 C
WARKENTINE, Theresa 1871 - 9 June 1955 D "Wife of Fred Warkentine"
WARTHA, Mary 1885 mother - 27 Feb 1967 C
Antony 1905 brother - 1918 C
Joanna T 1873 mother - 1901 C
Lawrence 1871 father - 1955 C
WARTHA, Joanna 1875 - 13

77

WARTHA (continued)
Mar 1968 A
Michael 1877 - 16 July
1950 A
Elizabeth C 1917 - 1922 A
WARTHA, Joseph 1886 - 5
Jan 1961 A
Katharine 1887 - 1978 A
Bertha 1889 - 1911 A (Nee:
Deka)
Joseph 1867 - 1924 A
Stephen 1860 - 1918 A
Anna 1895 - 7 Sept 1973 A
(D Kronewitter same lot)
WAS, John 1880 - 25 Aug
1948 C
WAS, Mary 1886 - 8 Mar
1942 D
Maryanna 1847 - 1937 D
WASOCKI, James 1938 - 31
July 1939 C
WAWRZON, Stella 1883 - 30
Aug 1945 A "Died at Jo-
liet, IL"
John -no dates- A (Salomea
Hojnacki same lot)
WAWRZYNCZAK, Jakob
1864 father - 1937 F
Marya 1870 mother - 22
Mar 1957 F
Henry P 13 Dec 1936 - 27
Jan 1937 F (James R
Slane same lot)
WAWRZYNIAK, Leokadya
1880 - 1939 F
Jan 1877 - 12 Nov 1942 F
Kate 1884 - 22 Aug 1939 F
WAWRZYNIAK, Frank 1866
father - 1915 C
Stella 1872 mother - 1940 C
Leon P 28 June 1894 - 28
Nov 1956 C "IN Pfc 875
Aero Repair Sq WWI"
WCISEL, Joseph no date -
1920 A (Jacob, Helen,
Leo, & Joseph Janowiak;

WCISEL (continued)
William & Michael North;
Michael Baloun; & Helen
Hosinski same lot)
WEBER, John J 1856 - 31
Mar 1950 C
WEBER, Joseph 1868 - 11
Oct 1940 F
WEGENKE, Frances 1861
mother - 1927 E (Nee:
Thilman)
Michael 1854 father - 1906
E
WEGER, A 1873 - 2 Oct
1953 F
WEGER, R 1884 - 10 Feb
1954 C
WEGERBAUER, Wilma 1869
- 3 Apr 1946 E
WEGNER, Maryanna no date
- 21 Mar 1892 D
Ludwig 1845 - 1908 D
Maryann 1861 - 1932 D (Jo-
seph Wagner same lot)
WEISE, Irving E 1895 - 8
Feb 1969 -
WELCHES, Joseph 1882 - 2
Apr 1964 B
WELCHES, John 1875 - 23
Mar 1958 C
WELSH, H K 1890 - 18 Nov
1947 B "Died in Chicago,
IL"
WENDERSKI, Helena 25 Dec
1897 - 7 Nov 1920 D
Joseph 1856 - 26 Feb 1939
D
Eva no date - 11 Aug 1929
D
WENSLAW (See: WIN-
SLOW), Florentyna no
date - 3 Sept 1912 E
(Stanislaw, Wladyslaw,
Genowefa, & Pelegia So-
sinski same lot)
WENTLAND, (See: WET-

78

WENTLAND (continued)
LANT), Julia B Cylka 5
Sept 1902 - 1978 F (Nee:
Tuligowski)
Joseph L 1892 - 1928 F
WENTLAND, John J 5 Oct
1891 - 6 May 1912 A
"Chief Mech Btry F 4 Fld
Arty Fort D Russel, WY"
John 1868 father -1928 A
Josephine 1866 mother -
1927 A
WENTLAND, Frank 1889 -
26 Sept 1920 A
Ann 1857 - 28 May 1900 A
(Nee: Rosna)
Peter 19 Feb 1845 - 25 July
1912 A
George 1876 - 11 Mar 1948
A
Dorothy 1899 - 20 Sept 1949
A
WERWINSKI, Michael 8 Sept
1853 - 17 July 1887 A
Note: Michael was first
husband of Amlia Kaiser
who then married Michael
Beczkiewicz. Amelia is
interred at St Joseph
Polish Cemetery with
Michael Beczkiewicz
WESOLEK, Anna 9 Feb 1892
- 18 Jan 1918 F
Thomas L 1882 - 7 Nov
1946 F
WESOLOWSKI, John F 1870
father - 1915 A
Bridget M 1875 mother -
1958 A (Nee: Sledzykow-
ski)
Stanislaw -no dates- A
Stanislawa -no dates- A
WESOLOWSKI, Martha 15
Jan 1882 wife - 28 Jan
1958 A (Nee: Witkowski)
Marion S 8 June 1872 - 19

WESOLOWSKI (continued)
Feb 1937 A "Co F 157 Inf
Spanish American War"
WESOLOWSKI, Wladyslaw
25 Feb 1884 - 8 June 1912
E (Nikodem, Maryanna,
Nick, & Julianna Nowinski
same lot)
WETLANT (See: WENT-
LAND), Michalina -no
dates- D (Nee: Buczkow-
ski)
Karul 1859 - 2 Dec 1906 D
"Parents" (Martin & An-
gela Andrzejewski same
lot)
WHITE, Joseph E 1895 - 5
Jan 1969 -
WHITE, Lafayette 1861 - 24
Mar 1950 C
WHITE, Frank 1871 - 7 Dec
1950 B
WIECZOREK, John P 1854 -
13 May 1938 G
Piotr 1893 - 19-- G
Elzbieta 1850 - 1917 G
Jadwiga 1895 - 1908 G
WIECZOREK, Mary 1871 -
1937 (with Picture) F
(Nee: Kiszka)
John J 1870 - 20 July 1953
F (Jan, Jadwiga, & Joseph
Witkowski; & John T Trz-
cina same lot)
WIECZOREK, Frank 1871 -
1925 C
Agnes 1881 - 16 Apr 1945 C
Casimir no date - 1902 C
Leo no date - 1903 C
Sylvester 1907 - 1908 C
WIECZORKOWSKI, Theo-
dore G 1913 - 1979 E
Mollie T 1913 - 6 Sept 1970
E
Wojciech 1903 - 1927 E
WIEGIEL, Paul - Memorial

WIEGIEL (continued)
buried - nothing legible
except "Co G 6th --- D
WILCZYNSKI, John 1884 -
27 Apr 1946 F
WILHELM, Oscar 1874 - 26
Sept 1946 C
Mary 1863 - 22 Dec 1940 C
WILLIAMS, Margaret 1872 -
12 Oct 1949 C
WIMSATT, Lillian 1904 - 1
Mar 1961 A
WINCEK, Elizabeth 1890
mother - 29 Dec 1967 C
Frank 1884 father - 26 May
1948 C
WINCEK, Teofilia Makowski
1911 - 11 Mar 1939 H
(Petronella Pietrzak &
Jozef Makowski same lot)
WINCEK, Joseph 1886 father
- 31 May 1965 C
Rose 1913 daughter - 19--
C
Rose 1889 mother - 15 Feb
1969 C
Rose 1911 baby - 1913 C
Carl 26 Mar 1926 - 8 Oct
1969 C "IN Pfc Inf WWII"
WINGETT, Elizabeth no date
- 19 June 1957 C
WINKLER, Sadie 1890 - 13
Sept 1960 A
Genevieve 1887 - 27 Apr
1966 A
WINKLER, Edward 1886 - 7
May 1958 B
WINNICKI, Lucian 1905 -
1937 C
Walter Jr 1915 - 1923 C
Walter 6 Nov 1868 - 21 Feb
1952 C
Pelegia 1876 - 17 Jan 1941
C (Nee: Trok)
WINSLOW (See: WEN-
SLAW), Bridget 1905 - 19

WINSLOW (continued)
May 1958 A
WISHIN, Ethel 1868 - 1 Nov
1948 C
Antony 1865 - 15 June 1938
C
WISNIEWSKI, Antony J 6
June 1886 - 19 July 1961
E "IN Pfc 16 Depot Bri-
gade WWI"
Josephine 1886 - 6 Apr
1957 E (Nee: Piasecki)
Frank R 1887 - 6 June 1946
E
Agnes 1849 mother - 1909
E (Nee: Sobol)
John 1851 father - 1898 E
Aloysius no date - 1908 E
WISNIEWSKI, Richard F
1880 - 1916 A (Marie
Evans same lot)
WITKOWSKI, Jan 1889 -
1936 E
Jadwiga 1903 - 19-- E
Joseph son of Harriet -
1931 E (Mary & John
Wieczorek; & John Trz-
cina same lot)
WITKOWSKI, Franciszka
June 1854 - 1918 C
Wawrzyniec May 1852 -
1914 C
Mary 1877 - 3 Apr 1955 C
WITKOWSKI, Wojciech 1852
- Dec 1893 A (Ignacy &
Jozefa Micinski same lot)
WITUCKI, John Frank -no
dates- C
Walaria April 1883 - no
dates C (Michael Zwier-
zynski same lot)
WITUCKI, Katharine 1814 -
1893 D
Jan 1817 - 1904 D (Anna &
Stanislaw Krajewski same
lot)

WITUCKI, Stanislawa 1867 -
1908 A (Nee: Bucholtz)
V W 1862 father 1900 A
Helen 1891 - 1910 A (An-
zelm W, Veronica, Alo-
ysius F, & Constance
Przybysz same lot)
WITUCKI, Alicya Teighler
1912 - 1977 A
Bert A 1907 - 18 Nov 1957
A
WITUCKI, Andrzej 29 Nov
1856 - 26 Dec 1904 D
Agnieszka 26 Dec 1862 - 2
Nov 1920 D
Rev Kazimierz 6 Aug 1900
- 7 Nov 1957 CSC D
(Richard C Balka same
lot)
WITUCKI, Andrzej father -no
dates- C
Katarzyna 1858 - 1946 C
WITUCKI, Antony 13 June
1864 - 15 Nov 1947 C
Frances 1867 - 2 Jan 1948
C (Nee: Hanyzewski)
WOELFUL, Pelegia 1868 -
18 July 1942 D
W O L F, Wilma 1885 - 12
Dec 1971 A
W O L F, Joseph 1872 - 22
Dec 1957 A
WOLF, Joseph D 1868 - 14
Jan 1944 C
W O L F, Mary C 1882 - 11
Aug 1945 G
WOLFE, C 1875 - 11 Dec
1955 C
Ralph 1902 - 17 May 1948
C
WOJCIECHOWSKI, Jozefa
no date - 11 Nov 1910 A
(Jan & Joanna Cybart
same lot)
WOJCIECHOWSKI, Helen -
1866 mother - 1922 C

WOJCIECHOWSKI (cont.)
Joseph 1866 father - 1921 C
WOJCIECHOWSKI, Marcy-
anna -no dates- C
WOJCIECHOWSKI, Eleanora
1888 - 23 Nov 1961 C
Wladyslaw 1880 - 30 Apr
1948 C
WOJCIECHOWSKI, Andrew
1857 - 1891 D (Joseph &
Anna Putz same lot)
WOJCIECHOWSKI, no name
no date son - 15 Nov 1926
F
WOJTALEWICZ, Rozalia
1847 - 23 Dec 1945 E
Antoni 1845 - 1906 E
WOLTMAN, Mary 1879 - 25
Nov 1951 C
Frank 1873 - 30 Jan 1965 C
WOLTMAN, Henrietta -no
dates- grandmother E (no
name Zgodzinski; Helen,
Mary, & John Redling;
Josephine & Bert Magiera;
& S Dean Dombkiewicz
same lot)
WOODKA, Andrew W 1881 -
2 Feb 1942 C
Frances 1846 mother - 1918
C (Nee: Napieralski)
Andrew Sr 1841 father -
1888 C
WOODKA, Louis S 1905 - 4
Feb 1982 C
Pauline 1883 - 19 Dec 1949
C (Nee: Sudrovech)
Roman 1874 - 14 Feb 1967
C
WOODKA, Joseph H 15 Apr
1910 - 19 Apr 1970 E
Ann M 2 Nov 1910 - no date
E
WOODWARD, Minnie 1883 -
9 Apr 1973 -
WORONOWICZ, Marya 16

WORONOWICZ (continued)
July 1857 mother - 3 Feb
1914 A
Wladyslaw 1850 father - no
date A
WOZNIAK, Ludwik 13 May
1901 - 20 Nov 1915 A
Joseph 13 Nov 1874 - 7 Mar
1955 A
Julia 13 Sept 1880 - 31 July
1968 A
WOZNIAK, Stella 19 Sept
1876 - 1 June 1963 C
Joseph 13 Sept 1872 - 11
Jan 1947 C
Albert T 14 Mar 1906 Son -
20 Apr 1979 C
WOZNIAK, Marcyanna 1851
- 2 Feb 1934 C (Nee:
Wichlacz)
Jan 1842 - 1935 C
WOZNIAK, no name -no
dates- D (Helen Broden
same lot)
WOZNIAK, Jacob 1840 -
1927 D (Antony, Leon, &
Joseph Wyremblewski; &
Mary Ornat same lot)
WOZNIAK, Helen 1885
mother - 1934 F (Nee:
Romsicki)
Jacob 1883 father - 1917 F
(John Romsicki same lot)
WOZNIAK, Teofilia 5 Mar
1861 - 20 May 1907 F
(Nee: Nowicki)
Steve 1865 - 25 Mar 1949 F
WOZNIAK, Rozalia 1875
mother - 1937 F (Nee:
Nowacki)
Vincent 1865 father - 6 Feb
1943 F
Wanda 1896 daughter - 17
Dec 1957 F
Ignacy 1896 son - 1919 F
(Michael Nowacki same

WOZNIAK (continued)
lot)
WOZNIAK, Helena 1861 -
1914 E
Franciszek 1884 - 1903 E
Wladyslaw 1858 - 1929 E
Walter 1886 - 1974 E (John
& Agnes Graczol same lot)
WOZNY, Casimir L 1898
father - 1979 E
Gladys A 1911 mother - 9
Dec 1969 E
WROBEL, Agnes J 1881 - 13
Dec 1963 D
Peter 1876 - 26 Dec 1962 D
Maryann 1880 - 5 Feb 1953
D
WROBEL, John 1906 - 23
Aug 1906 F
WROBLEWSKI, Jan J 1865 -
14 May 1954 A
Eleanor V 1874 - 22 July
1956 A (Nee: Sopczynski)
Frank X 1904 - 1981 A (Jo-
zef, Jan, & Anna Sopc-
zynski same lot)
WROBLEWSKI, Marie Sipotz
1902 - 1979 C
WROBLEWSKI, no name in-
fant - 21 Apr 1942 D
Franciszka 1878 - no date
D
WROBLEWSKI, Andrzej
1853 - 1890 D
Jozef 1883 - 1892 D
Anastasia 28 Feb 1860 - 10
July 1933 D (Nee: Ko-
walski)
WROBLEWSKI, Walenty no
date father - 30 Apr 1895
D
Marcin -no dates- D
Jozefa 1849 mother - 29
Apr 1944 D
WROBLEWSKI, Joseph 1884
father - 6 May 1957 D

WROBLEWSKI (continued)
Joe 1907 son - 13 May 1940
D
Anna 1883 mother - 20 Nov
1951 D (Nee: Palicki)
(Szymon & Konstancya
Palicki; Bertha Miller; &
Joseph & Regina Sta-
chowiak same lot)
WROBLEWSKI, Frank 1899
- 31 Jan 1972 -
WRZESZCZ, Marcin -no
dates- C
Jozefa -no dates- C (Mary,
Antony, & Helen Kopc-
zynski same lot)
WUTHRICH, Geraldine 1900
- 19 Jan 1969 - "Died at
Dowagiac, MI; wife of
Charles C Wuthrich"
WYREMBLEWSKI, Anton 12
Oct 1901 - 20 Apr 1924 D
Leon 1897 - 1924 D
Joseph B 3 July 1903 - 14
Jan 1980 D "Pvt US Army
WWII"
Michael 1873 - 1922 D
(Jacob Wozniak & Mary
Ornat same lot)
YAGER, John S 1892 - 6 July
1966 E
YANDEL, Ronald 1 month
old - 22 May 1941 C
YARSDORFER, John W 1864
- 19 July 1938 A
Frank 1859 - 25 July 1935
A
Catharine 1854 - 25 Nov
1935 A
YOUNG, Rev James 1902 - 9
Oct 1946 Community
Cemetery ND
YOUNGERMAN, Flora 1876
- 27 Aug 1954 B
Daniel 1876 - 18 July 1949
B

ZABLOCKI, Laura 1872 - 4
Apr 1919 A
ZACHAREK, Jan 5 Feb 1846
- Jan 1890 -
no name 1878 - no date -
ZAKASZEWSKI, Frances
1877 - 1926 A (Vincent,
Jan, & Maryanna Niez-
godski same lot)
ZAKOCS, M 1877 - 19 Jan
1954 A
ZAKROWSKI, Boleslaw 1885
husband - 1912 C
Amelia 1859 mother - 17
Mar 1919 C
Julian 1849 father 1896 C
Joseph Frank no date - 11
Jan 1929 C "IN Pvt 2 Regt
US Marines"
Josephine Zaworski 1889 -
20 Nov 1945 C "Wife of
Joseph Zaworski"
ZAKRZEWSKI, Malwina
1925 - 1929 C
ZALAS, Victoria 1871 - 1
June 1950 C (Nee: Stem-
pinski)
Michael 15 Aug 1869 - 13
May 1927 C
Teodor 9 July 1881 - 15 Jan
1918 C
Stanislaw 17 Mar 1897 - 19
Jan 1917 C
Jan 23 May 1893 - 19 Nov
1925 C
John P no date - 19 Sept
1925 C "WI Pvt 52 Eng"
ZALUDAK, J 1886 - 9 Nov
1954 Community Cemetery
ND
ZAMBRZNY, Josephine 8
Dec 1856 - 17 Apr 1898 C
(Boleslaw Jaworski same
lot)
ZANGERLE, Mary 1869 - 21
Dec 1946 F

ZANGERLE (continued)
Mark baby - 13 Mar 1968 F
ZATARGA, Frank 1876 father
- 10 July 1950 C
Mary 1880 mother - 23 Sept
1961 C
Sylvester 17 Dec 1915 - 8
Apr 1962 C "IN T/Sgt Med
Corps WWII"
Edward 1915 - 12 Apr 1962
C
ZBOROWSKI, Rev Antony
1860 - 1890 B "Pastor of
St Stanislaw Kostka Ro-
man Catholic Church of
Terre Coupe, IN" (Plaque
on north side of Chapel)
ZEITHAML, W 1878 - 9 Jan
1940 A
Marie J 1880 - 25 Apr 1952
A
ZEITHAML, Anthony 1881 -
19 June 1938 G
Caroline 1880 - 23 July
1969 G
ZEITLER, Margaret 1874 -
25 Apr 1960 A
ZGODZINSKI, no name
mother -no dates- E
no name father -no dates-
E (Helen, Mary, & John
Redling; Josephine & Bert
Magiera; S Dean Dombkie-
wicz; & Henrietta Wolt-
man same lot)
ZGODZINSKI, Wanda 1895 -
1899 F
Martin 1867 - 21 Apr 1949
F
Anna 1867 - 25 Apr 1965 F
(Andrew, Michalena, &
Clara Kosmatka same lot)
ZIELINSKI, Franciszek 26
Nov 1855 father - 5 Mar
1913 D
Agnieszka 1857 mother -

ZIELINSKI (continued)
1937 D
Anastzya -no dates- D
Maryanna -no dates- D
Franciszek -no dates- D
(Alex Szymanowski same
lot)
ZIELINSKI, Joseph J 1890 -
8 June 1971 E
Lenia Lee 1951 infant - 16
Dec 1951 E
M infant - 15 June 1953 E
ZIELINSKI, Wladyslaw 6 Jan
1893 - 16 Nov 1895 F
no name 1859 mother -
1916 F
ZILKOWSKI, no names 2 in-
fants male and female -
18 Aug 1948 D
ZIMMERMAN, Johanna
1863 - 17 July 1941 A
Bernhard 1867 - 29 Nov
1948 A
ZMUDZINSKI, Jan -no
dates- E
ZOSS, E 1877 - 3 July 1956
H
ZUMMER, Simon J 1898 - 2
Jan 1970 -
ZWIERZYNSKI, Jozefa 1848
mother - no date C (Nee:
Pianowski)
Michael 1852 - no date C
(Walaria & John Witucki
same lot)

INDEX

CHOLEWCZYNSKI, Agnieszka 68
CHROBOT, Mamie 63
CHUDZICKI, Katarzyna 73
    Magdelene 60
CHWALEK, Maryanna 14
CIEGIELSKI, Michael 63
    Sophie 63
CIESIELSKI, Blanche 39
    Catharine 59 Florence 39
    Lucya 39 Stella 39
CIESIOLKA, Eleanor 63
    Franciszek 31 Harriet T 9
    Mary 63 Pelegia 31
CLAYTON, Clara H 63
COLLNER, Josephine A
    Hack 3
COOK, Richard Daniel 19 37
    68
CURTIS, Theresa E 70
CWIKLINSKI, Stella 7
CYBART, Jan 81 Joanna 81
CZAJKOWSKI, Niespodziany
    50
CZANOWSKI, Joseph 18
    Julia K 18
DASZYNSKI, Salomea 68
DEKA, Anna 50 Bertha 78
    John 50 Marta 50
DOBRZYKOWSKI, Hattie 29
    Mary 37 Wladyslaw 48
DOBSKI, Lottie 38
DOMBKIEWICZ, S Dean 43
    61 81 84
DOMBROWSKI, Sophie 66
DOMINSKI, Felix 16 72
    Frances 72
DONARSKI, Apolonia 12
DRAJUS, Andrew 33
    Josephine 33 Julia 72
DREJER, Sophia K 42
DUDEK, Jan 40
EARL, Thomas A 15
EGIERSKI, Apolonia 26
    Josephine 22
EVANS, John W 16 Marie 80

FABIAN, Katalin 2 Stephen L
    2 Steve 2
FAY, Rose 75
FEZY, Joseph 41 Joseph J
    52
FILIPIAK, Mary 54
FILL, Henrietta 14 72
    Michael 16
FRAHLER, Michael 17
FRANCISZEK, Helen 21
FREDERICKS, Emery 50
    Emery A Jr 50
FRYDRYCH, Constance 47
GARY, Casimir 40 Elaine 40
GEABLER, Mary M 12 Walter F 12
GETTKE, Victoria 27 28
GIERSZ, Helen 41 Jacob 41
    Walentyna 22
GIERZYNSKI, Anna 49 Mary
    54
GINTER, Anna 42 Antonina
    42
GISH, Frances 22 Stephan K
    68 Stephen K 10 37
GLUCH, Bertha 36
GNOTH, Anna M 21 Ellen 21
    Mary 57 Michael J 21 William 21
GOLATA, Anna 21
GONSIOROWSKI, Elge D 57
    Helen 57 Hilary C 20 Irene
    Marie 40 Mary 57 Pelegia
    52 Rose 69 Sylvester 40 57
GORACZEWSKI, Walter 66
GORSKI, Elizabeth C 66
GRABAREK, Franciszka 42
GRABARZ, Anna 72
GRABOWSKI, Anna 19 Ferdinand 53 Matthew 19
    Sophie 53
GRACZOL, Agnes 82 John 82
GRAMS, Augusta 64 Joanna 3
    Josephine 3 Max J 3
    Patrich 22
GRAMZA, Catharine 5 Ed-

GRAMZA (continued)
ward 72 Rose 72
GRANS, Jan 22
GRANT, Frederich F 22
GREGA, Anna 71 Paul 71
GRONTKOWSKI, Frances 22
Frank 22 Josephine 22
GROSCH, Helen (Lena) 30
Lena 30
GRUSZKA, Frances C 44
GRUSZYNSKI, Jozef 19 Magdalina 19
GRZEGOREK, Leokadya 42
43
GRZESK, Jadwiga M 26
Lottie 24
GRZEZINSKI, Maryanna 63
GUDAJTYS, Maryanna 68
Wincenty 68
GUZICKI, Helen Luzny 42
Stanley 23
HABITZKI, Josephine 47
HAJDUCKI, Anne Kurek 39
HANYZEWSKI, Frances 81
John 40 49
HATHAWAY, Bessie 30
HAZINSKI, Antony 40
HERMAN, Josephine 67
HOJNACKI, Salomea 78 Walter 25
HORKA, Stanislawa 59
HORVATH, Paul 36
HOSINSKI, Anthony W 36
Apolonia 36 Helen 3 28 52
78 Ignac 26 Joanna 21
Leokadya 57 Mary 21
Nicodem F 36 Stanislawa
57
HUDAK, Stella 57
HUMBERGER, Adolph 3 Martha 3
JAGLA, Anna 61
JAGODZINSKI, Stanislaw 35
JANKOWSKI, Franciszka 63
Julia A 29 Mary 23
JANOWIAK, Helen 3 52 78

JANOWIAK (continued)
Jacob 3 52 78 Joseph 3 26
78 Josephine 52 Leo 3 52
78 Tadeusz 43 Thadeusz
64
JANOWSKI, Catharine 61
Joanna 61 Leokadya 34
Michael 61 Mieczyslaw 34
Nellie S 69
JARECKI, Katharine 69
JASKOWIAK, Blase 42
Frances 42 Stanley 42
JAWORSKI, Boleslaw 83
Cecelia 17 Frances 34 Jan
2 Lottie 5 Maryanna 2
Pelegia 2
JEGIER, Katharine 29
JENCZAK, Agnes 23
JULEK, Helen H 43
KACZMAREK, Josephine 24
Jozef 74
KAISER, Amlia 79
KALAJMAJSKI, Wanda 51
KALAMAJA, Anna 3 Sophia 8
KALAMAJSKI, Alex 30
Hattie 50
KALEWICZ, Anna 27
KALMAN, Charles 54
Charles J 54 Elizabeth 54
Paul 54 Victoria 54
KALOLINSKI, Frances 28
KAMAN, Mary Rose 37
KAMINSKI, Eliguis 10
KARESZEWSKI, Marcyanna
22
KASZA, Mary 68
KAZMIERCZAK, Anna C 3
KAZMIERSKI, Mary 23
KENDZIORSKI, Agnes 50
Angela G 42 Anna 11
KIERAN, John J 70 Mary 70
KINDT, Leon T 12
KINOWSKI, Konstanty 74
KISZKA, Mary 79
KIZER, Helen 26
KLADUSZ, John 32

87

KLAJBOR, Helen 59
KLEWIN, Anna 12
KLOS, Katarzyna 38
KLUSZYNSKI, Lottie 41
KLYSZ, Jozefa 14 Michael 14
KOBECKI, Pelegia M 56
KOCZAN, Catharine 33
    Joseph 33 Michael 33
KOCZOROWSKI, Mike 33
KOLACZYNSKI, Tekla 3
KOLCZYNSKI, Angeline 11
    Anna 74 Elanor 64 Eleanor
    60 Franciszek 42 Jan 42
    Stanislaw 74
KOLUPA, Michael 29
KOMASINSKI, Katarzyna 50
    Rose Fay 67
KOMINOWSKI, Rose 38
KONCZAN, Agnes 23
KOPCZYNSKI, Antony 83
    Helen 83 Mary 83
KORNOWICZ, Ludwika 28
    Wladyslaw 28
KORPAL, Antony J 40
KOSINSKI, Catharine 32
KOSMATKA, Andrew 84
    Clara 84 Michalena 84
KOTECKI, Frank 44 Helen 44
    Max 44 Wladyslaw 44
KOTOLINSKI, Eleanore 39
KOWALEK, Martha 24 25
    Wanda 59
KOWALSKI, Anastasia 82
    Anna 74 Antonina 26
    Bronislawa 55 Frances
    Podelwitz 60 Frances Rad-
    licki 58 Jozef 47 Mag-
    delena 26 Mary 60 61
    Marya 23 Peter 47 Rozalie
    B 26
KRAJEWSKI, Anna 80
    Stanislaw 80
KRAKOWSKI, Josephine 31
KRECZMER, Mary 21
KRIEGER, Agnes 20 Frances

KRIEGER (continued)
    68
KROLL, Mamie 62
KRONEWITTER, D 78
KRUK, Ladislaus 10 Ladys-
    law 19 68 Mary 10 19 56
    68
KRUZEL, Mary 13 14
KRZESZEWSKI, Mary J 35
    Veronica 23
KRZYCHOWSKI, Estell
    Szlanfucht 72
KRZYZANIAK, Frances 9
KUBIAK, Hattie R 6 Helen C
    6 Martin 38 Mary A 22
    Pauline G 40 Prakseda 38
    Rose 38 Stephen H 6
KUBISZEWSKI, Katarzyna 48
KUCHARSKI, Wladyslawa 9
KUJAWA, Rozalia 26
KUJAWSKI, Agnes 69 An-
    tonette 59 62 73 Antonette
    Laskowski Tajkowski 73
    Helen 59 Josephine M 28
    Martin 39 59 62 73 Rose
    58 Valentina 62
KUREK, Jennie 18 Joseph J
    24 Stanley 67
KUSH, Anna 32 Mary 23
KWIATKOWSKI, Josephine
    53 Martin 5 Mary 5 13
KWILINSKI, Josephine 57 58
LA GRUE, Kitty 58
LAGOCKI, Ignatius 59
    Maryanna 52
LASECKI, Amelia 70 Steven
    70
LASICKI, Amelia 6 Steven 6
LASKOWSKI, Antonette 38
    39 Antony 20 Apolonia 57
    Balbina 66 Elge D 20
    Joseph J 18 K 2 Leonard
    20 Pauline G 18
LATOSINSKI, Anton 26
    Elizabeth 26 Katarzyna 36
LECHNOROWICZ, Christian

LECHNOROWICZ (cont.)
3 Edward L 3 John 3
LEDA, Stella Michor 47
LEONARD, Josephine 19
LESECKI, Emelia 72 73
LESZCZ, Helen 57
LEWANDOWSKI, Antonina
72 Stephen 72
LISIECKI, Salomea 3
LISZEWSKI, Michalena 63
LIWOSZ, Wiktorya 48
LUCZKOWSKI, Joseph 16 52
Leokadya 52
LUDWICZAK, Frank 5 51
Rose 5 51
LUKASIEWICZ, Angela G 42
LUKASZEWSKI, James 29
Konstancya 37
LUKOWSKI, Clara 50
LUZNY, Alex 23 Antonina
Ginter 19 Boleslaw 19
Bruno 30 Clara B 19
George 30 Hattie 23 Mar-
tha 71 Paul P 23 Pauline
23 Roman 23 Sophie 30
Wanda 19
MACHOWIAK, Agnieszka 41
MAGIERA, Bert 14 61 81 84
Josephine 14 61 81 84
MAJEWSKI, Wladyslawa 34
MAKIELSKI, 28 64 Damazy
48 Josephine 64
MAKOWSKI, Frances 41
Joanna 71 Jozef 57 80
Valaria 58
MALLON, James 44
MANUSZAK, Rose 12
MARCINIAK, Henry 44
MARCINKOWSKI, Antoni 69
Antonina 69
MARKIEWICZ, Frank 44
Helen E 35 Joseph 35
Katharine 35
MARSHALL, Alex 30 Nellie
30 Victoria 5
MARTINSKI, Rose 13

MARUSZEWSKI, Frances 60
Stanislaw 60 Wojciech 60
MAZUKIEWICZ, Bertha J
Merrick 25
MAZUREK, Anna 5
MAZURKIEWICZ, Lottie 75
McHALLECK, Stanley 47
MEZYKOWSKI, Helen Ann
36
MICHALEK, Chester 46
MICHOCZA, Anna 13
MICHOR, Maryanna 40 Stella
40 Wojciech 40
MICINSKI, Ignacy 80 Jozefa
80 Konstancya 66
MILLER, Bertha 55 69 83
Lewis V 55
MINDYKOWSKI, 41
MNICHOWSKI, Antonina 7
Helen 28 Martha 38
Pelegia 10 Stanislaw 66
Stanislawa 66 Walerya 59
MOLLOY, Frank 48
MOZYNSKI, Franciszek 13
Stanislawa 13
MROSZKIEWICZ, Helen 43
Peter 43
MULNER, Elizabeth 19
MYSZKA, Michal 67
NAGY, J 24
NAPIERALSKI, Frances 81
NAWROCKI, Salomea 33
NEJMAN, Apolonia 66
NIEDBALSKI, Agnes 17 John
17 Leonard 61 Stella 32
Sylvester 61
NIEDZIELSKI, Ignacy 12
Marta 12
NIEMIER, Peter 56 Peter F
50
NIESPODZIANY, Clara 42
Josphine 42 Steve 42
NIEWIADOMY, Maryanna 5
42 Piotr 5 42 Rose 42
NIEZGODSKI, Bertha 44
Hattie 55 Jadwiga 18

NIEZGODSKI (continued)
Jan 83 Kazimiera 73
Maryanna 83 Pauline 40
Victoria 62 63 Vincent 83
NITKA, Constance 68
NIVEN, Edward 51
NORTH, Michael 3 26 28 78
William 3 78 Wm 26 28
NOWACKI, Katarzyna 39
Michael 82 Rozalia 82
NOWAK, Aniella 67 Anna 7
Eligius 60 Julia 60 Mary
73 Stanley 60
NOWAKOWSKI, Lillian 16
42
NOWICKI, Teofilia 82
NOWINSKI, Julianna 79
Maryanna 79 Nick 79
Nikodem 79
OBARSKI, Frank B 54 Helena
54 Julia 54
OBER, Antony 21 Edward 21
Mary 21 Sophie 21 Victor
21
OGNISZAK, Marcin 58
Napomucena 58
OGURKIEWICZ, A J 53 W A
53
ORNAT, Mary 82 83
OTOLSKI, Amelia 61 Eleanor
61 Eleanora 67 Joseph F
54 Michael L 61 67 Vic-
toria 21
PACESNY, Joanna 14
PACZESNY, Mary H 43
PAEGE, Alexander 53 Cle-
ment 53
PALICKI, Anna 41 83 Bertha
47 Frances 37 Helen 47
Jozefa 51 Katarzyna 51
Konstancya 47 69 83
Leokadya 7 Prakseda 60
Regina C 69 Stanislawa 60
Stanley 47 Szyman 47
Szymon 69 83 Wilhemina
60

PARYZ, Rozalea 69
PASZEK, Joseph 5 Mary 5
Mary Pilarski 5
PASZKIET, Leo 55
PAWLAK, Victoria 30 31
PETERSON, Charles 2 Julia
2 Mary J 2
PIANOWSKI, Jozefa 84
PIASECKI, Agnes 58 Antony
58 Frances 57 Joseph 58
Josephine 80 Mary J 34
PIECHOCKI, Michael 50
Wladyslawa 50
PIENIASZKIEWICZ, Joseph
D 20
PIENIAZKIEWICZ, Jozefa
20
PIERZYNCKI, Marya 26 John
J 57
PIETRZAK, John 57
Petronella 44 80
PILARSKI, Anna 53 54
Katarzyna 13 Mary 55
Wladyslawa 44
PINKOWSKI, Antonette 62
POCZEKAJ, Lottie 18 19
PODELWITZ, Anna 35
Augustine 60
POLICINSKI, Adeline S 53
POULIN, Flora 77
PRAWAT, Antonette 42 John
58 William 58
PRZESTWOR, John 68
PRZYBLINSKI, John Jr 39
PRZYBYLINSKI, Helen 59
John Jr 73 John Sr 59
Michael 59
PRZYBYSZ, Aloysius F 81
Anzelm W 81 Constance
81 Lottie S 55 Veronica 81
PRZYGOCKI, Felik 64 Felix
34 Teresa 64 Theresa 34
PULASKI, Jan 55 Prakseda
55
PULCINSKI, Martha 17
PUTZ, Anna 81 Joseph 81

RADAJ, Marya 45
RADOMSKI, Amelia 54 67
Telesfor 67 Telesfore 54
RAFINSKI, Anna 67 Francis
67 Mary B 67
RAJDER, Frank 67
RAJSKI, Anna 72 Bertha 72
Catharine 72
RAJTER, Antoni 4 Antonina
4 Jan 4 Michael 4 Wladys-
lawa 4
RAYSKI, Joseph V 29
REDLING, Helen 14 43 81 84
John 14 43 81 84 Mary 14
43 81 84
REED, Edith 44
REIDER, Conrad 37 Maire 37
Margaret 37
ROBCZYNSKI, Mary M 20
ROMSECKI, Joseph 9
ROMSICKI, Helen 82 John 62
82 Victoria 62
ROSIECH, Rozalia 70
ROSNA, Ann 79
ROWINSKI, Sophie 49
ROYTEK, Barbara 28
Michalina 75
ROZANSKI, Magdelina 75
ROZEK, Josephine 72
ROZEWICZ, Mary Ciegielski
8 9 Peter 63
ROZPLOCHOWSKI, Apolonia
35 Franciszka 64
Maryanna 27
ROZWARSKI, Mary 9
RUDYNSKI, Stella E 10
RUSIEWICZ, Anna 23
RUSZKOWSKI, Czeslaw 63
RUTKOWSKI, Joephine 64
Michal 64
RUTOWSKI, Josephine 43
Michael 28 43
RYBICKI, Francizska 4
RYCHLEWSKI, Katarzyna 34
60
SABERNIAK, John 28 43 64

SABERNIAK (continued)
Josephine 28 43 64
SCHROFF, Marlene S 14
SECHOWSKI, Gertrude 3
Hattie 19
SECULA, Frances 7
SIERADZKI, Suzanna 50
SKARICH, Anton 66
SKOLECKI, Rozalia 52
SKOLOWSKI, Wojciech 68
SKONIECKI, Katarzyna 21
SLANE, James R 78
SLEDZIKOWSKI, Alex 48
Frances F 48 Maryanna 48
Roman J 48
SLEDZYKOWSKI, Bridget M
79
SLISZ, Anton 66
SLOTT, Martin 75
SMIECINSKI, Blondine 54
Joseph 54
SMOGER, Antoni 49
Maryanna 49
SMUCINSKI, Blondine 61
Joseph 61
SOBCZAK, Josephine 61
SOBOL, Agnes 80
SOPCZYNSKI, Anna 82
Eleanor V 82 Jan 82 Jozef
82
SOSINSKI, Geonwefa 78
Pelegia 78 Stanislaw 78
Wladyslaw 78
SOWALA, Lawrence 10 19 37
SPYCHALSKI, Agnieszka 51
Andrzej 51 Joseph 59
Salomea 51 Stephen 51
STACHOWIAK, Antony 31
Bartholomew 69 Bernice 2
Bertha 1 Jan 1 Joseph 47
55 83 Katarzyna 1 Martin
31 Mary W 31 Maryanna
31 Regia 47 Regina 55 83
STASIAK, Jacob 20 Maryanna
20
STEMPIERSKI, Franciszka

STEMPIERSKI (continued)
71
STEMPIN, Joseph 44
STEMPINSKI, Victoria 83
STETZ, Marya 66
STRANTZ, Antonina 23
 Frances 32 Mary 32
STRUCK, Frances 40 John 40
STRUG, Anna 40
STULTS, Genevieve
 Szczechowski 72
STYPCZYNSKI, Mary 28
SUDROVECH, Pauline 81
SUPERCINSKI, Hattie 72
 Michalena 72
SUPERCZYNSKI, Eleanor 22
SWEDA, Leokadya 32
SYPNIEWSKI, Bronislawa 33
SZAMECKA, Pelegia 15
SZCZAPINSKI, Frances 14
 16 Stanley 14 16
SZCZECHOWSKI, Anna 70
 Genevieve V 70 Karolny 70
 Peter Paul 70
SZCZYPIORSKI, Peter 41
SZEWCZYK, Julia 22
SZLANFUCHT, Alex 72 Ber-
 tha 61 Jan 38 Jozefa 38
 Ludwig 38 Waleria 38
SZOTYNSKI, Josephine 55
SZUDROWICZ, Constance 13
SZULCZEWSKI, Lottie 71
 Walter 71
SZUMSKI, Angela 1
SZYBOWICZ, Anna 64 An-
 tonina 67 Catharine 50
 Joseph S 1 Mary 1 Marya
 50
SZYMANOWSKI, Franciszek
 84
SZYMANSKI, Franciszka 42
SZYMCZAK, Frances 3
 Frank 3
SZYMKOWIAK, Katharine 44
SZYNSKI, Franciszka 24
TABERSKI, Mary K 7

TABERSKI (continued)
 Maryanna 7 67 Pelegia 7
 Wladyslaw 7 67
TAJKOWSKI, E 39 59 J 39 S
 59 Wojciech 39
THILMAN, Frances 78 Lil-
 lian 34
THOMAS, Anna 2 Ruth J 2
TOBALSKI, Mary 19
TOBOLSKI, Jacob 32
TOMASZEWSKI, Agnieszka
 33
TOROK, A 75 Gyorgy 30 Joan
 Marie 75 M 75 Rose 30
TORZEWSKI, Franciszka 28
 Joseph 75 Leokadya 44
 Mary 34
TROK, Pelegia 80
TRZCINA, John 80 John T 79
TRZCINSKI, Sophie G 67
TSCHIDA, Elizabeth 70
TULIGOWSKI, Jacob 63
 Julia B 11 79
URBANSKI, Mikolaj 76
VASCIL, Andrew 76
WAGEMAN, Edward 77
WAGNER, Joseph 78
WALINSKI, Augusta 42
WARKENTINE, Fred 77
WARTHA, Anna 37 Bertha 37
 Joseph 37 Katharine 37
 Stephen 37
WAWRZON, John 25
 Salomea 25 Stella 25
WAWRZYNCZAK, Henry P
 66 Jakob 66 Mary 66
WAWRZYNIAK, Julia 55
WCISEL, J 28 Joseph 26 52
 Seph 3
WEGNER, Ludwig 77
 Maryanna 77
WENSATT, Lillian K 13
WENSLAW, Florentyna 68
WENTLAND, Joseph L 11
 Julia 36
WESOLOWSKI, Julia K 12

WESOLOWSKI (continued)
Tillie 3 41 Wladyslaw 52
WETLANT, Karul 2
Michalina 1 2
WICHLACZ, Marcyanna 82
WIECZOREK, John 75 80
Mary 75 80 Stella 57
WINCEK, Teofilia Makowski
44 Theofilia Makowski 57
WISNIEWSKI, Hedwige 39
Johanna 37 Richard F 16
WITKOWSKI, Jadwiga 79
Jan 75 79 Jawiga 75
Joseph 79 Martha 79 Woj-
ciech 47
WITUCKI, Agnieszka 2
Andrzej 2 Anne 10 Con-
stance 59 Helen 59 Jan 36
Jennie 28 Joanna 28 John
84 Kasimierz 2 3 Katar-
zyna 36 Veronica 59
Walaria 84 Wiktorya 46
WOJCIECHOWCKI, Jozefa
11 Andrew 60 Antonina 38
WOLTMAN, Constance 51
Helen 14 Henrietta 43 61
84 Sally 56
WOODKA, Anna 7 Maryanna
66 Wladyslawa 52
WOZNIAK, 6 Bernice 13
Helen 63 Jacob 54 63 83
Rose 22 Rozalia 52 Stella
17 Wincenty 52
WOZNICKI, Walter 21
Wladyslaw 21
WROBLEWSKI, Anna 47 55
69 Eleanor 68 Jan 68
Joseph 47 55 69 Stanis-
lawa 48 Wladyslawa 56
WRZESZCZ, Jozefa 34 Mar-
cin 34 Mary 34
WUTHRICH, Charles C 83
WYREMBLEWSKI, Antony
54 82 Joseph 82 Joseph B
54 Leon 54 82
ZAKASZEWSKI, Frances 51

ZAKRZEWSKI, Salomea 56
ZALAS, Jadwiga 58
ZAWORSKI, Joseph 83
Rozalia 58
ZGODZINSKI, 14 43 61 81
ZIELINSKI, Agnieszka 73
Franciszek 73 Valentyna
59
ZWIERZYNSKI, Michael 80

www.ingramcontent.com/pod-product-compliance
Lightning Source LLC
Chambersburg PA
CBHW060807110426
42739CB00032BA/3129